March 1, 2013

The Honorable John A. Boehner
Speaker of the House of Representatives
Washington, D.C. 20515

Dear Mr. Speaker:

Enclosed please find the Office of Management and Budget (OMB) Report to the Congress on the sequestration for fiscal year (FY) 2013 required by section 251A of the Balanced Budget and Emergency Deficit Control Act, as amended (the "Joint Committee sequestration"). This report provides calculations of the amounts and percentages by which various budgetary resources are required to be reduced, and a listing of the reductions required for each non-exempt budget account.

In August 2011, as part of the Budget Control Act of 2011 (BCA), bipartisan majorities in both the House of Representatives and Senate voted for sequestration as a mechanism to compel the Congress to act on deficit reduction. The threat of destructive across-the-board cuts under the BCA was intended to drive both sides to compromise. Yet, a year and a half has passed, and the Congress still has failed to enact balanced deficit reduction legislation that avoids sequestration.

As a result of the Congress's failure to act, the law requires the President to issue a sequestration order today canceling $85 billion in budgetary resources across the Federal Government for FY 2013. Specifically, OMB calculates that, over the course of the fiscal year, the sequestration requires a 7.8 percent reduction in non-exempt defense discretionary funding and a 5.0 percent reduction in non-exempt nondefense discretionary funding. The sequestration also requires reductions of 2.0 percent to Medicare, 5.1 percent to other non-exempt nondefense mandatory programs, and 7.9 percent to non-exempt defense mandatory programs.

Because these cuts must be achieved over only seven months instead of 12, the effective percentage reductions will be approximately 13 percent for non-exempt defense programs and 9 percent for non-exempt nondefense programs.

The cuts required by sequestration will be deeply destructive to national security, domestic investments, and core Government functions. While the Department of Defense will shift funds where possible to minimize the impact on war-fighting capabilities and critical military readiness, sequestration will result in a reduction in readiness of many non-deployed units, delays in investments in new equipment, cutbacks in equipment repairs and needed facilities maintenance, disruptions in military research and development efforts, significant reductions in weapons programs, and furloughs of most civilian employees for a significant amount of time. Sequestration will also undermine nondefense investments vital to economic growth, threaten the safety and security of the American people, and cause severe harm to programs that benefit the middle class, seniors, and children. According to analysis by outside experts, sequestration would reduce real GDP growth for 2013 by 0.5 to 0.7 percentage points were it to continue for the rest of the calendar year.

The Joint Committee sequestration is a blunt and indiscriminate instrument. It was never intended to be implemented and does not represent a responsible way for our Nation to achieve deficit reduction.

On multiple occasions, the President has proposed comprehensive and balanced deficit reduction plans to avoid sequestration. The President and Congress, working together, have already reduced the deficit by $2.5 trillion. The President has been clear that he is willing to make tough choices to reach an agreement on further deficit reduction. The Administration continues to stand ready to work with the Congress to enact balanced deficit reduction legislation that replaces sequestration and puts the Nation on a sound long-term fiscal path.

Sincerely,

Jeffrey D. Zients
Deputy Director for Management

Enclosure

Identical Letter Sent to the President of the Senate

OMB REPORT TO THE CONGRESS
ON THE JOINT COMMITTEE SEQUESTRATION
FOR FISCAL YEAR 2013

March 1, 2013

OMB REPORT TO THE CONGRESS
ON THE JOINT COMMITTEE SEQUESTRATION
FOR FISCAL YEAR 2013

The Balanced Budget and Emergency Deficit Control Act, as amended (BBEDCA), 2 U.S.C. § 901a, requires the Office of Management and Budget (OMB) to calculate, and the President to order on March 1, 2013, reductions in budgetary resources triggered by the failure of the Joint Select Committee on Deficit Reduction to propose, and the Congress to enact, legislation to reduce the deficit by $1.2 trillion (Joint Committee sequestration). This report provides OMB's calculations of the percentage and dollar amount of the reduction for each non-exempt budget account and an explanation of the calculations.

OMB calculates that the Joint Committee sequestration requires a 7.8 percent reduction in non-exempt defense discretionary funding and a 5.0 percent reduction in non-exempt non-defense discretionary funding. The sequestration also imposes reductions of 2.0 percent to Medicare, 5.1 percent to other non-exempt nondefense mandatory programs, and 7.9 percent to non-exempt defense mandatory programs.

Basis for Calculations

Discretionary Appropriations. As of the date of this report, no full-year regular appropriations bills have been enacted for fiscal year (FY) 2013. Instead, all agencies are operating under the Continuing Appropriations Resolution, 2013 (CR), Pub. L. 112-175. In addition, the Disaster Relief Appropriations Act, 2013 (Hurricane Sandy supplemental), Pub. L. 113-2, provided supplemental funding to various agencies for Hurricane Sandy relief and recovery efforts. Accordingly, as required by sections 251A(7)(A) and 253(f)(2) of BBEDCA, OMB's estimates for the level of sequestrable budgetary resources and resulting reductions assume that budget accounts with discretionary appropriations are funded at the annualized level provided by the CR, plus funding provided by the Hurricane Sandy supplemental and any funding enacted as advance appropriations for FY 2013. Unless another amount is specified by the CR, the annualized level equals the FY 2012 enacted appropriations, including changes in mandatory programs, net of any recurring rescissions, and increased by 0.612 percent pursuant to section 101(c) of the CR.[1] Spending authority from offsetting collections is only increased by the 0.612 percent when that spending authority is used to determine the annualized level. Amounts designated in the CR for Overseas Contingency Operations (OCO)/Global War on Terrorism (GWOT), and amounts incorporated in the CR by reference to the Disaster Relief Appropriations Act, 2012, Pub. L. 112-77, do not receive the 0.612 percent increase. As provided by section 101(b) of the CR, whenever an amount designated for OCO/GWOT pursuant to section 251(b)(2)(A) of BBEDCA in either the Department of Defense Appropriations Act, 2012 (division A of Pub. L. 112-74) or in the Military Construction and Veterans Affairs and Related Agencies Appropriations Act, 2012 (division H of Pub. L. 112-74) differs from the amount in the President's FY 2013 Budget request, the annualized level equals the amount in the President's FY 2013 Budget request. The CR levels are also adjusted for any transfers mandated by law.

Unobligated Balances in the Defense Function. Pursuant to section 255(e) of BBEDCA, unobligated balances in the defense function are sequestrable budgetary resources. The majority of estimated unobligated balances in the defense function are in Department of Defense accounts. In general, for multiyear accounts, the Department of Defense estimated unobligated balances as of March 1, 2013, by reducing unobligated balances as of December 31, 2012, by a historically-based estimate of obligations from prior year funds in January and February.

---

[1] Information about OMB's calculation of the amounts appropriated by the CR can be found in OMB Bulletin 12-02, which is available online at *http://www.whitehouse.gov/sites/default/files/omb/bulletins/fy2012/b12-02.pdf*.

Direct Spending. Estimates of sequestrable budgetary resources and outlays for budget accounts with direct spending are equal to the current law baseline amounts contained in the President's FY 2013 Budget, adjusted for the effects of legislation enacted since the Budget was transmitted. Two changes with the largest effect on the amount of sequestrable direct spending—providing for a zero percent update for Medicare payments to physicians under the Sustainable Growth Rate formula for calendar year 2013, and extending Emergency Unemployment Compensation (EUC) through the end of 2013—were enacted in the American Taxpayer Relief Act of 2012 (ATRA), Pub. L. 112-240.

Special Sequestration Rules. The Joint Committee sequestration order is not an order under section 254 of BBEDCA.[2] Accordingly, as set forth in this report, the special rules in section 256 that apply only to a sequestration order issued under section 254 do not apply to the Joint Committee sequestration, except to the extent those rules are otherwise made applicable by another provision of law. Section 251A(7)(A) of BBEDCA does not include any such provision for discretionary spending; as a result, in calculating the reduction in discretionary spending required by the Joint Committee sequestration, this report does not apply the special rules in section 256 that apply only to a sequestration order issued under section 254. The special rules in section 256 do, however, apply to the reduction in direct spending required by the Joint Committee sequestration, pursuant to the explicit direction in section 251A(8) of BBEDCA.

Federal Administrative Expenses. Under section 256(h) of BBEDCA, Federal administrative expenses are subject to sequestration pursuant to an order issued under section 254 "without regard to any exemption, exception, limitation, or special rule which is otherwise applicable." For the reasons set forth in the preceding paragraph, for the Joint Committee sequestration, this rule applies only to Federal administrative expenses that constitute direct spending. BBEDCA does not define "administrative expenses." For purposes of this report, "administrative expenses" for typical Government programs are defined as the object classes for personnel compensation, travel, transportation, communication, equipment, supplies, materials, and other services. For Government programs engaging in commercial, business-like activities, administrative expenses constitute overhead costs that are necessary to run a business, and not expenses that are directly tied to the production and delivery of goods or services.

American Taxpayer Relief Act of 2012. In addition to the changes to direct spending mentioned above, this report reflects three changes to the calculation of the Joint Committee sequestration required by ATRA. Section 901(a) reduced the amount of the FY 2013 sequestration by $24 billion, which was paid for by $12 billion of revenue increases and $12 billion in total reductions to the discretionary spending limits for FYs 2013 and 2014. Section 901(c) delayed the date for submission of this report from January 2, 2013 to March 1, 2013. Section 901(e) altered the discretionary spending limits for FY 2013 for purposes of calculating the Joint Committee sequestration.

Calculation of Sequestration Percentages

Under section 251A of BBEDCA, the failure of the Joint Select Committee on Deficit Reduction to propose, and the Congress to enact, legislation to reduce the deficit by $1.2 trillion triggers automatic reductions in discretionary appropriations and direct spending to achieve the deficit reduction that the Joint Select Committee process was meant to achieve. As shown in Table 1, the total annual amount of deficit reduction required is specified by formula in section 251A(3), starting with the total reduction of $1.2 trillion required for FY 2013 through

---

[2] For further discussion, see the OMB Report Pursuant to the Sequestration Transparency Act of 2012 (STA Report) issued in September.

FY 2021, deducting a specified 18 percent for debt service savings, and then dividing the result by 9 to calculate the annual reduction of $109 billion for each year from FY 2013 to FY 2021. As discussed previously, ATRA lowered the amount of the reduction required for FY 2013 by $24 billion, leaving $85 billion to be achieved through sequestration. The annual reduction is split evenly between budget accounts in function 050 (defense function) and in all other functions (nondefense function), so that each function group will be reduced by $42.667 billion in FY 2013.

Table 1.   CALCULATION OF TOTAL ANNUAL REDUCTION BY FUNCTION
(In billions of dollars)

Joint Committee required savings	1,200.000
Deduct debt service savings (18%)	−216.000
Net programmatic reductions	984.000
Divide by 9 to calculate annual reduction	109.333
Reduction for FY 13 pursuant to section 901(a) of ATRA	−24.000
Net remaining programmatic reduction for FY 2013	85.333
Split 50/50 between defense and nondefense functions	42.667

Base for Allocating Reductions. The annual reduction is further allocated between discretionary and direct spending within each of the function groups in proportion to their share of total spending within the function group. The base for allocating reductions to discretionary appropriations is the discretionary spending limit for FY 2013 listed in section 251(c)(2) as revised by section 251A(2)(A), and as applied pursuant to section 901(e) of ATRA. For purposes of this report, the discretionary spending limits have not been revised to include adjustments pursuant to section 251(b)(2) for certain funding included in the CR and Hurricane Sandy supplemental because these adjustments cannot be made until OMB issues its Discretionary Final Sequestration Report for FY 2013 on March 27th pursuant to section 901(b) of ATRA. Pursuant to paragraphs (5) and (6) of section 251A, and consistent with section 6 of the Statutory Pay-As-You-Go Act of 2010, 2 U.S.C. § 935, the base for allocating reductions to budget accounts with direct spending is the sum of the direct spending outlays in the budget year and the subsequent year that would result from new sequestrable budget authority in FY 2013.

Sequestrable Base. Once the reductions are allocated between discretionary appropriations and direct spending using the bases above, the sequestration percentage for discretionary appropriations is obtained by dividing the discretionary reduction required by the discretionary sequestrable base, which is described above in the "Basis for Calculations" section. By statute, the discretionary sequestrable base differs from the base used to allocate the reductions between discretionary appropriations and direct spending. For discretionary defense programs, the sequestrable base equals total discretionary appropriations (including funding that would trigger cap adjustments), plus unobligated balances and funding financed by fees, minus exemptions. Except for funding for military personnel accounts, most discretionary defense funding is sequestrable.[3] For discretionary nondefense programs, the sequestrable base equals total discretionary appropriations (including funding that would

---

[3] Defense sequestrable budgetary resources include non-exempt new budget authority and unobligated balances carried over from prior fiscal years. Budgetary resources for military personnel accounts are exempt pursuant to section 255(f) of BBEDCA and the July 31, 2012 letter from OMB notifying the Congress of the President's intent to exempt military personnel accounts from sequestration, available at: _http://www.whitehouse.gov/sites/default/files/omb/legislative/letters/military-personnel-letter-biden.pdf_.

trigger cap adjustments) and funding financed by fees, adjusted to exclude funding for the Department of Veterans Affairs, Pell Grants, and other exempt amounts. For mandatory programs, the sequestrable base is the same as the mandatory base for allocating the reduction. Pursuant to sections 251A(8), 255, and 256 of BBEDCA, most mandatory spending is exempt from sequestration or, in the case of the Medicare program and certain health programs, is subject to a 2 percent limit on sequestration.

Defense Function Reduction

Table 2 shows the calculation of the sequestration percentages and dollar reductions required for budget accounts with discretionary appropriations or direct spending within the defense function. The calculation involves the following steps:

Step 1. Pursuant to section 251A(5), the total reduction of $42.667 billion is allocated proportionately between discretionary appropriations and direct spending. The total base is the sum of the FY 2013 revised discretionary spending limit for the security category[4] ($544 billion) and OMB's baseline estimates of sequestrable direct spending outlays in the defense function in FY 2013 and FY 2014 from new direct spending budget authority in FY 2013 ($0.662 billion). Discretionary appropriations comprise more than 99 percent of the total base in the defense function.

Step 2. Total defense function spending must be reduced by $42.667 billion. As required by section 251A(5)(A), allocating the reduction based on the ratio of the revised discretionary spending limit to the total base (the sum of the defense discretionary spending limit and sequestrable direct spending) yields a $42.615 billion reduction required for discretionary appropriations. Under section 251A(5)(B), the remaining $0.052 billion is the reduction required for budget accounts with direct spending.

Step 3. As required by section 251A(7)(A), the discretionary percentage reduction for FY 2013 is calculated by dividing the discretionary reduction amount calculated in step 2 ($42.615 billion) by the sequestrable budgetary resources ($549.325 billion) for budget accounts with discretionary appropriations in the defense function, which yields a 7.8 percent sequestration rate for budget accounts with non-exempt discretionary appropriations. A similar calculation is required by section 251A(8) for the sequestration of direct spending. Dividing the direct spending reduction amount ($0.052 billion) by the sequestrable budgetary resources ($0.662 billion) for budget accounts with direct spending yields a 7.9 percent sequestration rate for budget accounts with non-exempt direct spending.

Table 2. DEFENSE FUNCTION REDUCTION
(Dollars in billions)

		Discretionary	Direct Spending	Total
Step 1.	Base for allocating reduction	544.000	0.662	544.662
	Percentage allocation of reductions	99.88%	0.12%	
Step 2.	Allocation of total reduction	42.615	0.052	42.667
	Percentage allocation of reductions	99.88%	0.12%	
Step 3.	Sequestration percentages calculation:			
	Sequestrable base	549.325	0.662	
	Sequestration percentage	7.8%	7.9%	

---

[4] For purposes of this report, the "security category" means discretionary appropriations in budget function 050, National Defense, and "nonsecurity category" means discretionary appropriations other than in budget function 050.

Nondefense Function Reduction

Table 3 shows the calculation of the sequestration percentages and dollar reductions required for budget accounts with discretionary appropriations or direct spending within all other functions besides 050 (nondefense function). The calculation is more complicated than the calculation for the defense function due to a two percent limit on sequestration of Medicare non-administrative spending, a two percent limit on sequestration of community and migrant health centers (which applies only to mandatory funding for those programs), and a special rule for applying the sequestration to student loans. The calculation involves the following steps:

Step 1. Total spending in the nondefense function must be reduced by $42.667 billion. The portion of Medicare subject to the two percent limit is estimated to have combined FY 2013 and FY 2014 outlays of $567.340 billion[5] from FY 2013 budgetary resources, so a two percentage point reduction would reduce outlays by $11.347 billion, leaving a reduction of $31.320 billion to be taken from discretionary appropriations and other direct spending in the nondefense function.

Step 2. Pursuant to section 251A(6), the remaining reduction of $31.320 billion is allocated proportionately between discretionary appropriations and other direct spending in the nondefense function. The remaining base ($605.839 billion) is the sum of the FY 2013 revised discretionary spending limit for the nonsecurity category ($499.000 billion) and the remaining sequestrable direct spending base ($106.839 billion).[6] The latter amount equals OMB's 2013 Budget baseline estimates of total sequestrable direct spending outlays adjusted for legislation enacted since the Budget's transmittal ($674.179 billion), minus the portion of Medicare subject to the two percent limit ($567.340 billion) in the nondefense function in FY 2013 and FY 2014 from new direct spending budget authority in FY 2013. The discretionary spending limit accounts for 82.37 percent of the remaining base in the nondefense function, and direct spending accounts for 17.63 percent.

Applying these percentage allocations to the non-Medicare reduction required for programs in the nondefense function yields the reduction for discretionary appropriations ($25.798 billion) and for remaining direct spending ($5.522 billion).

Step 3. The sequestration for the mandatory portions of certain health programs is limited to two percentage points pursuant to sections 251A(8) and 256(e)(2). The portion of these two programs subject to the two percent limit is estimated to have combined FY 2013 and FY 2014 outlays of $1.344 billion from FY 2013 budgetary resources, so a two percentage point reduction would reduce outlays by $0.027 billion. Deducting these savings from the non-Medicare direct spending reduction leaves $5.495 billion to be taken by a uniform percentage reduction of the remaining sequestrable direct spending of $105.495 billion in the nondefense function.

Step 4. As required by section 251A(7)(A), dividing the discretionary reduction amount ($25.798 billion) calculated in step 2 by the sequestrable budgetary resources for discretionary appropriations ($511.785 billion) in the nondefense function yields an 5.0 percent sequestration rate for budget accounts with non-exempt discretionary appropriations.[7]

---

[5] As stated above, the Medicare base is higher than the amount stated in the STA Report due primarily to provisions in ATRA providing for a zero percent update for Medicare payments to physicians under the Sustainable Growth Rate formula for calendar year 2013.

[6] As stated above, the non-Medicare direct spending base is higher than the amount stated in the STA Report due primarily to a provision in ATRA extending EUC through the end of 2013.

[7] As stated above, the nondefense discretionary base is higher than the amount stated in the STA Report due primarily to the Hurricane Sandy supplemental.

The remaining reduction ($5.495 billion) to direct spending is applied as a uniform percentage reduction to the remaining budget accounts with sequestrable direct spending and by increasing student loan fees by the same uniform percentage, as specified in sections 251A(8) and 256(b). Each percentage point increase in the sequestration rate is estimated to result in $0.016 billion of savings in the direct student loan program. Solving simultaneously for the percentage that would achieve the remaining reduction when applied to both the remaining sequestrable direct spending ($105.495 billion) and to student loan fees yields a 5.1 percent reduction. This percentage reduction would yield savings of $0.082 billion in the direct student loan program and $5.413 billion from the remaining budget accounts with non-exempt direct spending.

Table 3. NONDEFENSE FUNCTION REDUCTION
(Dollars in billions)

		Discretionary	Direct Spending	Total
1.	Total reduction, excluding savings from Medicare 2% limit:			
	Medicare base subject to 2% limit		567.340	
	Total nondefense function reduction			42.667
	Reduce Medicare by 2%			−11.347
	Non-Medicare reduction amounts			31.320
2.	Allocate non-Medicare reduction:			
	Total base for allocating reduction	499.000	674.179	1,173.179
	Exclude Medicare (portion subject to 2% limit)		−567.340	−567.340
	Non-Medicare base	499.000	106.839	605.839
	Percentage allocation of non-Medicare base	82.37%	17.63%	
	Non-Medicare reduction amounts	25.798	5.522	31.320
	Percentage allocation of non-Medicare reduction	82.37%	17.63%	
3.	Savings from 2% limit on sequestration of other health programs*			
	Other health programs sequestrable base		1.344	
	Reduce other health programs by 2%		−0.027	
4.	Sequestration percentages calculation:			
	Remaining reduction amounts	25.798	5.495	
	Savings from uniform percentage reduction:			
	From 5.1% increase in student loan fee		0.082	
	From remaining sequestrable budget accounts	25.798	5.413	
	Sequestrable base for uniform percentage reduction	511.785	105.495	
	Sequestration percentage	5.0%	5.1%	
	Summary of reductions:			
	2% sequestration of Medicare		11.347	
	2% limit on sequestration of other health programs		0.027	
	Student loan fee increase		0.082	
	Uniform percentage reduction	25.589	5.380	
	Rounding	0.209	.033	
	Total reduction	25.798	16.869	42.667

* Includes funding for community and migrant health centers, and for Indian health services.

Reductions by Budget Account (Appendix)

The Appendix of this report sets forth the percentage and dollar amount of the reductions required for each budget account with sequestrable funding. Specifically, the Appendix shows the sequestrable budgetary resources in each budget account, the percentage reduction required for each sequestrable budgetary resource, and the resulting reduction. For illustrative purposes only, the Appendix shows the application of the same percentage reduction to each type of budgetary resource within a budget account. There is no requirement that sequestration be applied equally to each type of budgetary resource within a budget account. Section 256(k)(2) of BBEDCA requires that sequestration be applied equally at the program, project, and activity level within each budget account.

APPENDIX: SEQUESTRABLE BASE AND REDUCTIONS BY BUDGET ACCOUNT

(Fiscal year 2013; in millions of dollars)

Based on sections 251A, 255, and 256 of the Balanced Budget and Emergency Deficit Control Act of 1985 (BBEDCA), as amended

Percentages Used:
7.8 percent – Defense discretionary
7.9 percent – Defense mandatory
5.0 percent – Nondefense discretionary
5.1 percent – Nondefense mandatory

For illustrative purposes only, the Appendix shows the application of the same percentage reduction to each type of budgetary resource within a budget account. Pursuant to section 256(k)(2) of the Balanced Budget and Emergency Deficit Control Act of 1985, the sequestration must be applied equally at the program, project, and activity level, but need not be applied equally to each type of budgetary resource within a budget account.

Sequestrable Budgetary Resources and Reductions in Sequestrable Resources by OMB Account -- FY 2013

(Amounts in millions)

Agency / Bureau / Account / Function / BEA Category / Budgetary Resource	Sequestrable BA Amount	Sequester Percentage	Sequester Amount
Legislative Branch			
Senate			
001-05-0110 Salaries, Officers and Employees			
Nondefense Discretionary Appropriation	177	5.0	9
001-05-0123 Miscellaneous Items			
Nondefense Discretionary Appropriation	19	5.0	1
001-05-0126 Secretary of the Senate			
Nondefense Discretionary Appropriation	6	5.0	*
001-05-0127 Sergeant at Arms and Doorkeeper of the Senate			
Nondefense Discretionary Appropriation	132	5.0	7
001-05-0128 Inquiries and Investigations			
Nondefense Discretionary Appropriation	132	5.0	7
001-05-0130 Senators' Official Personnel and Office Expense Account			
Nondefense Discretionary Appropriation	399	5.0	20
001-05-0185 Office of the Legislative Counsel of the Senate			
Nondefense Discretionary Appropriation	7	5.0	*
001-05-0188 Congressional Use of Foreign Currency, Senate			
Nondefense Mandatory Appropriation	6	5.1	*
001-05-9911 Senate Items			
Nondefense Discretionary Appropriation	2	5.0	*
House of Representatives			
001-10-0400 Salaries and Expenses			
Nondefense Discretionary Appropriation	1,233	5.0	62
001-10-0488 Congressional Use of Foreign Currency, House of Representatives			
Nondefense Mandatory Appropriation	1	5.1	*
Joint Items			
001-11-0181 Joint Economic Committee			
Nondefense Discretionary Appropriation	4	5.0	*
001-11-0186 Joint Congressional Committee on Inaugural Ceremonies of 2013			
Nondefense Discretionary Appropriation	1	5.0	*
001-11-0190 Office of Congressional Accessibility Services			
Nondefense Discretionary Appropriation	1	5.0	*
001-11-0425 Office of the Attending Physician			
Nondefense Discretionary Appropriation	3	5.0	*
001-11-0460 Joint Committee on Taxation			
Nondefense Discretionary Appropriation	10	5.0	1
Office of Compliance			
001-12-1600 Salaries and Expenses			
Nondefense Discretionary Appropriation	4	5.0	*
Capitol Police			
001-13-0476 General Expenses			
Nondefense Discretionary Appropriation	63	5.0	3
001-13-0477 Salaries			
Nondefense Discretionary Appropriation	279	5.0	14

* denotes $500,000 or less.

Sequestrable Budgetary Resources and Reductions in Sequestrable Resources by OMB Account -- FY 2013

(Amounts in millions)

Agency / Bureau / Account / Function / BEA Category / Budgetary Resource			Sequestrable BA Amount	Sequester Percentage	Sequester Amount
Congressional Budget Office					
001-14-0100 Salaries and Expenses					
Nondefense	Discretionary	Appropriation	44	5.0	2
Architect of the Capitol					
001-15-0100 General Administration					
Nondefense	Discretionary	Appropriation	102	5.0	5
001-15-0105 Capitol Building					
Nondefense	Discretionary	Appropriation	36	5.0	2
001-15-0108 Capitol Grounds					
Nondefense	Discretionary	Appropriation	10	5.0	1
001-15-0123 Senate Office Buildings					
Nondefense	Discretionary	Appropriation	72	5.0	4
001-15-0127 House Office Buildings					
Nondefense	Discretionary	Appropriation	95	5.0	5
001-15-0133 Capitol Power Plant					
Nondefense	Discretionary	Appropriation	124	5.0	6
001-15-0155 Library Buildings and Grounds					
Nondefense	Discretionary	Appropriation	47	5.0	2
001-15-0161 Capitol Visitor Center					
Nondefense	Discretionary	Appropriation	21	5.0	1
001-15-0171 Capitol Police Buildings and Grounds					
Nondefense	Discretionary	Appropriation	22	5.0	1
001-15-1833 House Historic Buildings Revitalization Trust Fund					
Nondefense	Discretionary	Appropriation	30	5.0	2
001-15-4518 Judiciary Office Building Development and Operations Fund					
Nondefense	Mandatory	Borrowing authority	12	5.1	1
Botanic Garden					
001-18-0200 Botanic Garden					
Nondefense	Discretionary	Appropriation	12	5.0	1
Library of Congress					
001-25-0101 Salaries and Expenses, Library of Congress					
Nondefense	Discretionary	Appropriation	416	5.0	21
001-25-0102 Copyright Office: Salaries and Expenses					
Nondefense	Discretionary	Appropriation	16	5.0	1
001-25-0127 Congressional Research Service: Salaries and Expenses					
Nondefense	Discretionary	Appropriation	107	5.0	5
001-25-0141 Books for the Blind and Physically Handicapped: Salaries and Expenses					
Nondefense	Discretionary	Appropriation	51	5.0	3
Government Printing Office					
001-30-0201 Office of Superintendent of Documents: Salaries and Expenses					
Nondefense	Discretionary	Appropriation	35	5.0	2
001-30-0203 Congressional Printing and Binding					
Nondefense	Discretionary	Appropriation	91	5.0	5

Agency / Bureau / Account / Function / BEA Category / Budgetary Resource	Sequestrable BA Amount	Sequester Percentage	Sequester Amount
001-30-4505 Government Printing Office Revolving Fund			
Nondefense Discretionary Appropriation	1	5.0	*
Nondefense Mandatory Administrative expenses in otherwise exempt resources	2	5.1	*
Account Total	3		*
Government Accountability Office			
001-35-0107 Salaries and Expenses			
Nondefense Discretionary Appropriation	514	5.0	26
United States Tax Court			
001-40-0100 Salaries and Expenses			
Nondefense Discretionary Appropriation	51	5.0	3
Legislative Branch Boards and Commissions			
001-45-1801 Medicaid and CHIP Payment and Access Commission			
Nondefense Discretionary Appropriation	6	5.0	*
001-45-2973 United States-China Economic and Security Review Commission			
Nondefense Discretionary Appropriation	3	5.0	*
001-45-2975 Commission on International Religious Freedom			
Nondefense Discretionary Appropriation	3	5.0	*
001-45-2990 Capital Construction, Dwight D. Eisenhower Memorial Commission			
Nondefense Discretionary Appropriation	31	5.0	2
001-45-8148 Open World Leadership Center Trust Fund			
Nondefense Discretionary Appropriation	10	5.0	1
001-45-9911 Other Legislative Branch Boards and Commissions			
Nondefense Discretionary Appropriation	7	5.0	*

* denotes $500,000 or less.

(Amounts in millions)

Agency / Bureau / Account / Function / BEA Category / Budgetary Resource	Sequestrable BA Amount	Sequester Percentage	Sequester Amount
Judicial Branch			
Supreme Court of the United States			
002-05-0100 Salaries and Expenses			
Nondefense Discretionary Appropriation	73	5.0	4
002-05-0103 Care of the Building and Grounds			
Nondefense Discretionary Appropriation	8	5.0	*
United States Court of Appeals for the Federal Circuit			
002-07-0510 Salaries and Expenses			
Nondefense Discretionary Appropriation	30	5.0	2
United States Court of International Trade			
002-15-0400 Salaries and Expenses			
Nondefense Discretionary Appropriation	20	5.0	1
Courts of Appeals, District Courts, and other Judicial Services			
002-25-0920 Salaries and Expenses			
Nondefense Discretionary Appropriation	4,716	5.0	236
Nondefense Mandatory Appropriation	65	5.1	3
Account Total	4,781		239
002-25-0923 Defender Services			
Nondefense Discretionary Appropriation	1,037	5.0	52
002-25-0925 Fees of Jurors and Commissioners			
Nondefense Discretionary Appropriation	52	5.0	3
002-25-0930 Court Security			
Nondefense Discretionary Appropriation	503	5.0	25
002-25-5100 Judiciary Filing Fees			
Nondefense Mandatory Administrative expenses in otherwise exempt resources	80	5.1	4
Nondefense Mandatory Appropriation	194	5.1	10
Account Total	274		14
002-25-5101 Registry Administration			
Nondefense Mandatory Appropriation	1	5.1	*
Administrative Office of the United States Courts			
002-26-0927 Salaries and Expenses			
Nondefense Discretionary Appropriation	83	5.0	4
Federal Judicial Center			
002-30-0928 Salaries and Expenses			
Nondefense Discretionary Appropriation	27	5.0	1
United States Sentencing Commission			
002-39-0938 Salaries and Expenses			
Nondefense Discretionary Appropriation	17	5.0	1

* denotes $500,000 or less.

Agency / Bureau / Account / Function / BEA Category / Budgetary Resource	Sequestrable BA Amount	Sequester Percentage	Sequester Amount
Department of Agriculture			
Office of the Secretary			
005-03-9913 Office of the Secretary			
Nondefense Discretionary Appropriation	16	5.0	1
Departmental Management			
005-05-0117 Agriculture Buildings and Facilities and Rental Payments			
Nondefense Discretionary Appropriation	232	5.0	12
005-05-0500 Hazardous Materials Management			
Nondefense Discretionary Appropriation	4	5.0	*
005-05-9915 Departmental Administration			
Nondefense Discretionary Appropriation	86	5.0	4
Office of Communications			
005-06-0150 Office of Communications			
Nondefense Discretionary Appropriation	8	5.0	*
Office of Civil Rights			
005-07-3800 Office of Civil Rights			
Nondefense Discretionary Appropriation	21	5.0	1
Office of Inspector General			
005-08-0900 Office of Inspector General			
Nondefense Discretionary Appropriation	86	5.0	4
Office of Chief Economist			
005-09-0123 Office of the Chief Economist			
Nondefense Discretionary Appropriation	11	5.0	1
Office of the General Counsel			
005-10-2300 Office of the General Counsel			
Nondefense Discretionary Appropriation	40	5.0	2
National Appeals Division			
005-11-0706 National Appeals Division			
Nondefense Discretionary Appropriation	13	5.0	1
Economic Research Service			
005-13-1701 Economic Research Service			
Nondefense Discretionary Appropriation	78	5.0	4
National Agricultural Statistics Service			
005-15-1801 National Agricultural Statistics Service			
Nondefense Discretionary Appropriation	160	5.0	8
Agricultural Research Service			
005-18-1400 Salaries and Expenses			
Nondefense Discretionary Appropriation	1,102	5.0	55
005-18-8214 Miscellaneous Contributed Funds			
Nondefense Mandatory Administrative expenses in otherwise exempt resources	2	5.1	*
National Institute of Food and Agriculture			

* denotes $500,000 or less.

(Amounts in millions)

Agency / Bureau / Account / Function / BEA Category / Budgetary Resource	Sequestrable BA Amount	Sequester Percentage	Sequester Amount
005-20-0502 Extension Activities			
Nondefense Discretionary Appropriation	478	5.0	24
Nondefense Mandatory Appropriation	5	5.1	*
Account Total	483		24
005-20-1500 Research and Education Activities			
Nondefense Discretionary Appropriation	714	5.0	36
005-20-1502 Integrated Activities			
Nondefense Discretionary Appropriation	21	5.0	1
Animal and Plant Health Inspection Service			
005-32-1600 Salaries and Expenses			
Nondefense Discretionary Appropriation	822	5.0	41
Nondefense Discretionary Spending authority	18	5.0	1
Nondefense Mandatory Appropriation	266	5.1	14
Account Total	1,106		56
005-32-1601 Buildings and Facilities			
Nondefense Discretionary Appropriation	3	5.0	*
005-32-9971 Miscellaneous Trust Funds			
Nondefense Mandatory Administrative expenses in otherwise exempt resources	1	5.1	*
Food Safety and Inspection Service			
005-35-3700 Salaries and Expenses			
Nondefense Discretionary Appropriation	1,010	5.0	51
Nondefense Discretionary Spending authority	45	5.0	2
Account Total	1,055		53
005-35-8137 Expenses and Refunds, Inspection and Grading of Farm Products			
Nondefense Mandatory Administrative expenses in otherwise exempt resources	1	5.1	*
Grain Inspection, Packers and Stockyards Administration			
005-37-2400 Salaries and Expenses			
Nondefense Discretionary Appropriation	38	5.0	2
005-37-4050 Limitation on Inspection and Weighing Services Expenses			
Nondefense Mandatory Administrative expenses in otherwise exempt resources	1	5.1	*
Nondefense Mandatory Spending authority	40	5.1	2
Account Total	41		2
Agricultural Marketing Service			
005-45-2500 Marketing Services			
Nondefense Discretionary Appropriation	83	5.0	4
005-45-2501 Payments to States and Possessions			
Nondefense Discretionary Appropriation	1	5.0	*
005-45-5070 Perishable Agricultural Commodities Act Fund			
Nondefense Mandatory Appropriation	11	5.1	1
005-45-5209 Funds for Strengthening Markets, Income, and Supply (section 32)			
Nondefense Mandatory Appropriation	792	5.1	40
005-45-8015 Expenses and Refunds, Inspection and Grading of Farm Products			
Nondefense Mandatory Administrative expenses in otherwise exempt resources	4	5.1	*
Nondefense Mandatory Appropriation	4	5.1	*
Account Total	8		*
005-45-8412 Milk Market Orders Assessment Fund			
Nondefense Mandatory Spending authority	57	5.1	3

Sequestrable Budgetary Resources and Reductions in Sequestrable Resources by OMB Account -- FY 2013

(Amounts in millions)

Agency / Bureau / Account / Function / BEA Category / Budgetary Resource			Sequestrable BA Amount	Sequester Percentage	Sequester Amount
Risk Management Agency					
005-47-2707 Administrative and Operating Expenses					
Nondefense	Discretionary	Appropriation	75	5.0	4
005-47-4085 Federal Crop Insurance Corporation Fund					
Nondefense	Mandatory	Administrative expenses in otherwise exempt resources	58	5.1	3
Farm Service Agency					
005-49-0170 State Mediation Grants					
Nondefense	Discretionary	Appropriation	4	5.0	*
005-49-0171 Emergency Forest Restoration Program					
Nondefense	Discretionary	Appropriation	23	5.0	1
005-49-0600 Salaries and Expenses					
Nondefense	Discretionary	Appropriation	1,206	5.0	60
005-49-1140 Agricultural Credit Insurance Fund Program Account					
Nondefense	Discretionary	Appropriation	408	5.0	20
005-49-1336 Commodity Credit Corporation Export Loans Program Account					
Nondefense	Discretionary	Appropriation	7	5.0	*
005-49-2701 USDA Supplemental Assistance					
Nondefense	Discretionary	Appropriation	2	5.0	*
005-49-3304 Grassroots Source Water Protection Program					
Nondefense	Discretionary	Appropriation	4	5.0	*
005-49-3305 Reforestation Pilot Program					
Nondefense	Discretionary	Appropriation	1	5.0	*
005-49-3316 Emergency Conservation Program					
Nondefense	Discretionary	Appropriation	15	5.0	1
005-49-4336 Commodity Credit Corporation Fund					
Nondefense	Mandatory	Borrowing authority	6,460	5.1	329
005-49-5531 Agricultural Disaster Relief Fund					
Nondefense	Mandatory	Borrowing authority	1,372	5.1	70
005-49-8161 Tobacco Trust Fund					
Nondefense	Mandatory	Appropriation	960	5.1	49
Natural Resources Conservation Service					
005-53-1000 Conservation Operations					
Nondefense	Discretionary	Appropriation	833	5.0	42
Nondefense	Discretionary	Spending authority	9	5.0	*
		Account Total	842		42
005-53-1002 Watershed Rehabilitation Program					
Nondefense	Discretionary	Appropriation	15	5.0	1
005-53-1004 Farm Security and Rural Investment Programs					
Nondefense	Mandatory	Administrative expenses in otherwise exempt resources	108	5.1	6
Nondefense	Mandatory	Appropriation	3,249	5.1	166
		Account Total	3,357		171
005-53-1072 Watershed and Flood Prevention Operations					
Nondefense	Discretionary	Appropriation	180	5.0	9
005-53-3320 Water Bank Program					
Nondefense	Discretionary	Appropriation	8	5.0	*
Rural Development					

Sequestrable Budgetary Resources and Reductions in Sequestrable Resources by OMB Account -- FY 2013

(Amounts in millions)

Agency / Bureau / Account / Function / BEA Category / Budgetary Resource	Sequestrable BA Amount	Sequester Percentage	Sequester Amount
005-55-0403 Salaries and Expenses			
Nondefense Discretionary Appropriation	183	5.0	9
Rural Utilities Service			
005-60-1230 Rural Electrification and Telecommunications Loans Program Account			
Nondefense Discretionary Appropriation	37	5.0	2
005-60-1232 Distance Learning, Telemedicine, and Broadband Program			
Nondefense Discretionary Appropriation	38	5.0	2
005-60-1980 Rural Water and Waste Disposal Program Account			
Nondefense Discretionary Appropriation	506	5.0	25
005-60-2042 High Energy Cost Grants			
Nondefense Discretionary Appropriation	10	5.0	1
Rural Housing Service			
005-63-0137 Rental Assistance Program			
Nondefense Discretionary Appropriation	910	5.0	46
005-63-1951 Rural Community Facilities Program Account			
Nondefense Discretionary Appropriation	29	5.0	1
005-63-1953 Rural Housing Assistance Grants			
Nondefense Discretionary Appropriation	33	5.0	2
005-63-2002 Multifamily Housing Revitalization Program Account			
Nondefense Discretionary Appropriation	13	5.0	1
005-63-2006 Mutual and Self-help Housing Grants			
Nondefense Discretionary Appropriation	30	5.0	2
005-63-2081 Rural Housing Insurance Fund Program Account			
Nondefense Discretionary Appropriation	514	5.0	26
Rural Business_Cooperative Service			
005-65-1900 Rural Cooperative Development Grants			
Nondefense Discretionary Appropriation	25	5.0	1
005-65-1902 Rural Business Program Account			
Nondefense Discretionary Appropriation	75	5.0	4
005-65-1908 Rural Energy for America Program			
Nondefense Discretionary Appropriation	3	5.0	*
Nondefense Mandatory Appropriation	22	5.1	1
Account Total	25		1
005-65-2069 Rural Development Loan Fund Program Account			
Nondefense Discretionary Appropriation	11	5.0	1
005-65-2073 Energy Assistance Payments			
Nondefense Mandatory Appropriation	65	5.1	3
Foreign Agricultural Service			
005-68-2277 Public Law 480 Title I Direct Credit and Food for Progress Program Account			
Nondefense Discretionary Appropriation	3	5.0	*
005-68-2278 Food for Peace Title II Grants			
Nondefense Discretionary Appropriation	1,475	5.0	74
005-68-2900 Salaries and Expenses			
Nondefense Discretionary Appropriation	177	5.0	9
Nondefense Mandatory Appropriation	1	5.1	*
Account Total	178		9

* denotes $500,000 or less.

Agency / Bureau / Account / Function / BEA Category / Budgetary Resource			Sequestrable BA Amount	Sequester Percentage	Sequester Amount
005-68-2903 McGovern-Dole International Food for Education and Child Nutrition Program					
Nondefense	Discretionary	Appropriation	185	5.0	9
Food and Nutrition Service					
005-84-3505 Supplemental Nutrition Assistance Program					
Nondefense	Mandatory	Administrative expenses in otherwise exempt resources	93	5.1	5
005-84-3507 Commodity Assistance Program					
Nondefense	Discretionary	Appropriation	73	5.0	4
Nondefense	Mandatory	Appropriation	21	5.1	1
		Account Total	94		5
005-84-3508 Nutrition Programs Administration					
Nondefense	Discretionary	Appropriation	140	5.0	7
005-84-3510 Special Supplemental Nutrition Program for Women, Infants, and Children (WIC)					
Nondefense	Discretionary	Appropriation	6,659	5.0	333
Nondefense	Mandatory	Appropriation	1	5.1	*
		Account Total	6,660		333
005-84-3539 Child Nutrition Programs					
Nondefense	Mandatory	Administrative expenses in otherwise exempt resources	36	5.1	2
Nondefense	Mandatory	Appropriation	13	5.1	1
		Account Total	49		3
Forest Service					
005-96-1103 Capital Improvement and Maintenance					
Nondefense	Discretionary	Appropriation	430	5.0	22
Nondefense	Discretionary	Spending authority	16	5.0	1
		Account Total	446		22
005-96-1104 Forest and Rangeland Research					
Nondefense	Discretionary	Appropriation	298	5.0	15
Nondefense	Discretionary	Spending authority	2	5.0	*
		Account Total	300		15
005-96-1105 State and Private Forestry					
Nondefense	Discretionary	Appropriation	260	5.0	13
005-96-1106 National Forest System					
Nondefense	Discretionary	Appropriation	1,615	5.0	81
Nondefense	Discretionary	Spending authority	14	5.0	1
		Account Total	1,629		81
005-96-1115 Wildland Fire Management					
Nondefense	Discretionary	Appropriation	2,448	5.0	122
Nondefense	Discretionary	Spending authority	53	5.0	3
		Account Total	2,501		125
005-96-1119 Management of National Forest Lands for Subsistence Uses					
Nondefense	Discretionary	Appropriation	3	5.0	*
005-96-4605 Working Capital Fund					
Nondefense	Discretionary	Spending authority	3	5.0	*
005-96-5207 Range Betterment Fund					
Nondefense	Discretionary	Appropriation	3	5.0	*
005-96-5540 Stewardship Contracting Product Sales					
Nondefense	Mandatory	Appropriation	8	5.1	*

Agency / Bureau / Account / Function / BEA Category / Budgetary Resource	Sequestrable BA Amount	Sequester Percentage	Sequester Amount
005-96-9921 Forest Service Permanent Appropriations			
Nondefense Mandatory Administrative expenses in otherwise exempt resources	1	5.1	*
Nondefense Mandatory Appropriation	646	5.1	33
Account Total	647		33
005-96-9923 Land Acquisition			
Nondefense Discretionary Appropriation	74	5.0	4
Nondefense Mandatory Appropriation	9	5.1	*
Account Total	83		4
005-96-9974 Forest Service Trust Funds			
Nondefense Mandatory Administrative expenses in otherwise exempt resources	2	5.1	*
Nondefense Mandatory Appropriation	77	5.1	4
Account Total	79		4

Agency / Bureau / Account / Function / BEA Category / Budgetary Resource	Sequestrable BA Amount	Sequester Percentage	Sequester Amount
Department of Commerce			
Departmental Management			
006-05-0120 Salaries and Expenses			
Nondefense Discretionary Appropriation	57	5.0	3
006-05-0123 HCHB Renovation and Modernization			
Nondefense Discretionary Appropriation	5	5.0	*
006-05-0126 Office of the Inspector General			
Nondefense Discretionary Appropriation	29	5.0	1
Nondefense Discretionary Spending authority	1	5.0	*
Account Total	30		2
Economic Development Administration			
006-06-0125 Salaries and Expenses			
Nondefense Discretionary Appropriation	38	5.0	2
006-06-2050 Economic Development Assistance Programs			
Nondefense Discretionary Appropriation	221	5.0	11
Bureau of the Census			
006-07-0401 Salaries and Expenses			
Nondefense Discretionary Appropriation	255	5.0	13
Nondefense Mandatory Appropriation	30	5.1	2
Account Total	285		14
006-07-0450 Periodic Censuses and Programs			
Nondefense Discretionary Appropriation	638	5.0	32
Economic and Statistical Analysis			
006-08-1500 Salaries and Expenses			
Nondefense Discretionary Appropriation	97	5.0	5
International Trade Administration			
006-25-1250 Operations and Administration			
Nondefense Discretionary Appropriation	458	5.0	23
006-25-5521 Grants to Manufacturers of Worsted Wool Fabrics			
Nondefense Mandatory Appropriation	5	5.1	*
Bureau of Industry and Security			
006-30-0300 Operations and Administration			
Defense Discretionary Appropriation	34	7.8	3
Nondefense Discretionary Appropriation	67	5.0	3
Nondefense Discretionary Spending authority	1	5.0	*
Account Total	102		6
Minority Business Development Agency			
006-40-0201 Minority Business Development			
Nondefense Discretionary Appropriation	30	5.0	2
National Oceanic and Atmospheric Administration			
006-48-1450 Operations, Research, and Facilities			
Nondefense Discretionary Appropriation	3,289	5.0	164
Nondefense Mandatory Spending authority	6	5.1	*
Account Total	3,295		165
006-48-1451 Pacific Coastal Salmon Recovery			
Nondefense Discretionary Appropriation	65	5.0	3

Agency / Bureau / Account / Function / BEA Category / Budgetary Resource	Sequestrable BA Amount	Sequester Percentage	Sequester Amount
006-48-1460 Procurement, Acquisition and Construction			
Nondefense Discretionary Appropriation	2,013	5.0	101
006-48-1465 Medicare-eligible Retiree Health Fund Contribution, NOAA			
Nondefense Discretionary Appropriation	2	5.0	*
006-48-4316 Damage Assessment and Restoration Revolving Fund			
Nondefense Mandatory Appropriation	6	5.1	*
006-48-5139 Promote and Develop Fishery Products and Research Pertaining to American Fisheries			
Nondefense Mandatory Appropriation	16	5.1	1
006-48-5284 Limited Access System Administration Fund			
Nondefense Mandatory Appropriation	10	5.1	1
006-48-5362 Environmental Improvement and Restoration Fund			
Nondefense Mandatory Appropriation	1	5.1	*
U.S. Patent and Trademark Office			
006-51-1006 Salaries and Expenses			
Nondefense Discretionary Spending authority	2,951	5.0	148
National Institute of Standards and Technology			
006-55-0500 Scientific and Technical Research and Services			
Nondefense Discretionary Appropriation	580	5.0	29
006-55-0515 Construction of Research Facilities			
Nondefense Discretionary Appropriation	56	5.0	3
006-55-0525 Industrial Technology Services			
Nondefense Discretionary Appropriation	129	5.0	6
National Telecommunications and Information Administration			
006-60-0516 State and Local Implementation Fund			
Nondefense Mandatory Borrowing authority	69	5.1	4
006-60-0550 Salaries and Expenses			
Nondefense Discretionary Appropriation	46	5.0	2
006-60-8233 Public Safety Trust Fund			
Nondefense Mandatory Borrowing authority	105	5.1	5

Agency / Bureau / Account / Function / BEA Category / Budgetary Resource	Sequestrable BA Amount	Sequester Percentage	Sequester Amount
Department of Defense--Military Programs			
Operation and Maintenance			
007-10-0100 Operation and Maintenance, Defense-wide			
Defense Discretionary Appropriation	38,457	7.8	3,000
Defense Discretionary Unobligated balance in 050	748	7.8	58
Account Total	39,205		3,058
007-10-0104 United States Court of Appeals for the Armed Forces			
Defense Discretionary Appropriation	14	7.8	1
007-10-0105 Drug Interdiction and Counter-Drug Activities			
Defense Discretionary Appropriation	1,685	7.8	131
007-10-0107 Office of the Inspector General			
Defense Discretionary Appropriation	360	7.8	28
Defense Discretionary Unobligated balance in 050	4	7.8	*
Account Total	364		28
007-10-0111 Department of Defense Acquisition Workforce Development Fund			
Defense Discretionary Appropriation	107	7.8	8
Defense Discretionary Unobligated balance in 050	290	7.8	23
Account Total	397		31
007-10-0118 Overseas Contingency Operations Transfer Fund			
Defense Discretionary Unobligated balance in 050	10	7.8	1
007-10-0130 Defense Health Program			
Defense Discretionary Appropriation	33,528	7.8	2,615
Defense Discretionary Spending authority	971	7.8	76
Defense Discretionary Unobligated balance in 050	1,503	7.8	117
Account Total	36,002		2,808
007-10-0134 Cooperative Threat Reduction Account			
Defense Discretionary Appropriation	511	7.8	40
Defense Discretionary Unobligated balance in 050	222	7.8	17
Account Total	733		57
007-10-0462 Military Intelligence Program Transfer Fund			
Defense Discretionary Appropriation	313	7.8	24
007-10-0801 Foreign Currency Fluctuations			
Defense Discretionary Unobligated balance in 050	970	7.8	76
007-10-0810 The Department of Defense Environmental Restoration Accounts			
Defense Discretionary Appropriation	1,198	7.8	93
Defense Discretionary Unobligated balance in 050	7	7.8	1
Account Total	1,205		94
007-10-0811 Environmental Restoration, Formerly Used Defense Sites			
Defense Discretionary Appropriation	328	7.8	26
007-10-0819 Overseas Humanitarian, Disaster, and Civic Aid			
Defense Discretionary Appropriation	109	7.8	9
Defense Discretionary Unobligated balance in 050	65	7.8	5
Account Total	174		14
007-10-0833 Emergency Response Fund			
Defense Discretionary Unobligated balance in 050	214	7.8	17
007-10-0838 Support for International Sporting Competitions			
Defense Discretionary Unobligated balance in 050	10	7.8	1

* denotes $500,000 or less.

Sequestrable Budgetary Resources and Reductions in Sequestrable Resources by OMB Account -- FY 2013

(Amounts in millions)

Agency / Bureau / Account / Function / BEA Category / Budgetary Resource			Sequestrable BA Amount	Sequester Percentage	Sequester Amount
007-10-1106 Operation and Maintenance, Marine Corps					
Defense	Discretionary	Appropriation	9,643	7.8	752
007-10-1107 Operation and Maintenance, Marine Corps Reserve					
Defense	Discretionary	Appropriation	299	7.8	23
007-10-1804 Operation and Maintenance, Navy					
Defense	Discretionary	Appropriation	44,274	7.8	3,453
Defense	Discretionary	Unobligated balance in 050	15	7.8	1
		Account Total	44,289		3,455
007-10-1806 Operation and Maintenance, Navy Reserve					
Defense	Discretionary	Appropriation	1,369	7.8	107
007-10-2020 Operation and Maintenance, Army					
Defense	Discretionary	Appropriation	59,336	7.8	4,628
Defense	Discretionary	Unobligated balance in 050	84	7.8	7
		Account Total	59,420		4,635
007-10-2065 Operation and Maintenance, Army National Guard					
Defense	Discretionary	Appropriation	7,352	7.8	573
Defense	Discretionary	Unobligated balance in 050	1	7.8	*
		Account Total	7,353		574
007-10-2080 Operation and Maintenance, Army Reserve					
Defense	Discretionary	Appropriation	3,245	7.8	253
007-10-2091 Afghanistan Security Forces Fund					
Defense	Discretionary	Appropriation	5,749	7.8	448
Defense	Discretionary	Unobligated balance in 050	4,519	7.8	352
		Account Total	10,268		801
007-10-2096 Afghanistan Infrastructure Fund					
Defense	Discretionary	Appropriation	400	7.8	31
Defense	Discretionary	Unobligated balance in 050	69	7.8	5
		Account Total	469		37
007-10-3400 Operation and Maintenance, Air Force					
Defense	Discretionary	Appropriation	44,443	7.8	3,467
007-10-3740 Operation and Maintenance, Air Force Reserve					
Defense	Discretionary	Appropriation	3,415	7.8	266
007-10-3840 Operation and Maintenance, Air National Guard					
Defense	Discretionary	Appropriation	6,162	7.8	481
007-10-4965 Emergency Response					
Defense	Discretionary	Unobligated balance in 050	12	7.8	1
007-10-5188 Disposal of Department of Defense Real Property					
Defense	Discretionary	Appropriation	8	7.8	1
Defense	Discretionary	Unobligated balance in 050	55	7.8	4
		Account Total	63		5
007-10-5189 Lease of Department of Defense Real Property					
Defense	Discretionary	Appropriation	11	7.8	1
Defense	Discretionary	Unobligated balance in 050	71	7.8	6
		Account Total	82		6
007-10-5193 Overseas Military Facility Investment Recovery					
Defense	Discretionary	Unobligated balance in 050	2	7.8	*

Sequestrable Budgetary Resources and Reductions in Sequestrable Resources by OMB Account -- FY 2013

(Amounts in millions)

Agency / Bureau / Account / Function / BEA Category / Budgetary Resource			Sequestrable BA Amount	Sequester Percentage	Sequester Amount
007-10-9922 Miscellaneous Special Funds					
Defense	Mandatory	Appropriation	8	7.9	1
Defense	Mandatory	Unobligated balance in 050	17	7.9	1
		Account Total	25		2
Procurement					
007-15-0144 Mine Resistant Ambush Protected Vehicle Fund					
Defense	Discretionary	Unobligated balance in 050	600	7.8	47
007-15-0300 Procurement, Defense-wide					
Defense	Discretionary	Appropriation	5,130	7.8	400
Defense	Discretionary	Unobligated balance in 050	670	7.8	52
		Account Total	5,800		452
007-15-0350 National Guard and Reserve Equipment					
Defense	Discretionary	Unobligated balance in 050	217	7.8	17
007-15-0360 Defense Production Act Purchases					
Defense	Discretionary	Appropriation	171	7.8	13
Defense	Discretionary	Unobligated balance in 050	151	7.8	12
		Account Total	322		25
007-15-0380 Coastal Defense Augmentation					
Defense	Discretionary	Unobligated balance in 050	4	7.8	*
007-15-0390 Chemical Agents and Munitions Destruction, Defense					
Defense	Discretionary	Appropriation	1,564	7.8	122
Defense	Discretionary	Unobligated balance in 050	2	7.8	*
		Account Total	1,566		122
007-15-1109 Procurement, Marine Corps					
Defense	Discretionary	Appropriation	2,376	7.8	185
Defense	Discretionary	Unobligated balance in 050	1,180	7.8	92
		Account Total	3,556		277
007-15-1506 Aircraft Procurement, Navy					
Defense	Discretionary	Appropriation	17,871	7.8	1,394
Defense	Discretionary	Unobligated balance in 050	2,914	7.8	227
		Account Total	20,785		1,621
007-15-1507 Weapons Procurement, Navy					
Defense	Discretionary	Appropriation	3,234	7.8	252
Defense	Discretionary	Unobligated balance in 050	703	7.8	55
		Account Total	3,937		307
007-15-1508 Procurement of Ammunition, Navy and Marine Corps					
Defense	Discretionary	Appropriation	889	7.8	69
Defense	Discretionary	Unobligated balance in 050	103	7.8	8
		Account Total	992		77
007-15-1611 Shipbuilding and Conversion, Navy					
Defense	Discretionary	Appropriation	15,010	7.8	1,171
Defense	Discretionary	Unobligated balance in 050	7,459	7.8	582
		Account Total	22,469		1,753
007-15-1810 Other Procurement, Navy					
Defense	Discretionary	Appropriation	6,089	7.8	475
Defense	Discretionary	Unobligated balance in 050	1,320	7.8	103
		Account Total	7,409		578

* denotes $500,000 or less.

Sequestrable Budgetary Resources and Reductions in Sequestrable Resources by OMB Account -- FY 2013

(Amounts in millions)

Agency / Bureau / Account / Function / BEA Category / Budgetary Resource	Sequestrable BA Amount	Sequester Percentage	Sequester Amount
007-15-2031 Aircraft Procurement, Army			
Defense Discretionary Appropriation	5,858	7.8	457
Defense Discretionary Unobligated balance in 050	1,532	7.8	119
Account Total	7,390		576
007-15-2032 Missile Procurement, Army			
Defense Discretionary Appropriation	1,490	7.8	116
Defense Discretionary Spending authority	15	7.8	1
Defense Discretionary Unobligated balance in 050	231	7.8	18
Account Total	1,736		135
007-15-2033 Procurement of Weapons and Tracked Combat Vehicles, Army			
Defense Discretionary Appropriation	2,079	7.8	162
Defense Discretionary Spending authority	20	7.8	2
Defense Discretionary Unobligated balance in 050	751	7.8	59
Account Total	2,850		222
007-15-2034 Procurement of Ammunition, Army			
Defense Discretionary Appropriation	2,239	7.8	175
Defense Discretionary Spending authority	22	7.8	2
Defense Discretionary Unobligated balance in 050	299	7.8	23
Account Total	2,560		200
007-15-2035 Other Procurement, Army			
Defense Discretionary Appropriation	9,548	7.8	745
Defense Discretionary Spending authority	17	7.8	1
Defense Discretionary Unobligated balance in 050	3,501	7.8	273
Account Total	13,066		1,019
007-15-2093 Joint Improvised Explosive Device Defeat Fund			
Defense Discretionary Appropriation	1,675	7.8	131
Defense Discretionary Unobligated balance in 050	303	7.8	24
Account Total	1,978		154
007-15-3010 Aircraft Procurement, Air Force			
Defense Discretionary Appropriation	13,050	7.8	1,018
Defense Discretionary Unobligated balance in 050	9,753	7.8	761
Account Total	22,803		1,779
007-15-3011 Procurement of Ammunition, Air Force			
Defense Discretionary Appropriation	619	7.8	48
Defense Discretionary Unobligated balance in 050	112	7.8	9
Account Total	731		57
007-15-3020 Missile Procurement, Air Force			
Defense Discretionary Appropriation	5,944	7.8	464
Defense Discretionary Unobligated balance in 050	640	7.8	50
Account Total	6,584		514
007-15-3080 Other Procurement, Air Force			
Defense Discretionary Appropriation	20,271	7.8	1,581
Defense Discretionary Unobligated balance in 050	442	7.8	34
Account Total	20,713		1,616
Research, Development, Test, and Evaluation			
007-20-0400 Research, Development, Test and Evaluation, Defense-wide			
Defense Discretionary Appropriation	19,391	7.8	1,512
Defense Discretionary Unobligated balance in 050	1,145	7.8	89
Account Total	20,536		1,602

* denotes $500,000 or less.

Sequestrable Budgetary Resources and Reductions in Sequestrable Resources by OMB Account -- FY 2013

(Amounts in millions)

Agency / Bureau / Account / Function / BEA Category / Budgetary Resource			Sequestrable BA Amount	Sequester Percentage	Sequester Amount
007-20-0460 Operational Test and Evaluation, Defense					
Defense	Discretionary	Appropriation	189	7.8	15
Defense	Discretionary	Unobligated balance in 050	9	7.8	1
		Account Total	198		15
007-20-1319 Research, Development, Test and Evaluation, Navy					
Defense	Discretionary	Appropriation	17,909	7.8	1,397
Defense	Discretionary	Unobligated balance in 050	953	7.8	74
		Account Total	18,862		1,471
007-20-2040 Research, Development, Test and Evaluation, Army					
Defense	Discretionary	Appropriation	8,814	7.8	687
Defense	Discretionary	Unobligated balance in 050	793	7.8	62
		Account Total	9,607		749
007-20-3600 Research, Development, Test and Evaluation, Air Force					
Defense	Discretionary	Appropriation	26,695	7.8	2,082
Defense	Discretionary	Unobligated balance in 050	1,727	7.8	135
		Account Total	28,422		2,217
Military Construction					
007-25-0391 Chemical Demilitarization Construction, Defense-wide					
Defense	Discretionary	Appropriation	75	7.8	6
Defense	Discretionary	Unobligated balance in 050	2	7.8	*
		Account Total	77		6
007-25-0500 Military Construction, Defense-wide					
Defense	Discretionary	Appropriation	3,321	7.8	259
Defense	Discretionary	Unobligated balance in 050	2,493	7.8	194
		Account Total	5,814		454
007-25-0510 Department of Defense Base Closure Account 1990					
Defense	Discretionary	Appropriation	326	7.8	25
007-25-0512 Department of Defense Base Closure Account 2005					
Defense	Discretionary	Unobligated balance in 050	601	7.8	47
007-25-0803 Foreign Currency Fluctuations, Construction					
Defense	Discretionary	Unobligated balance in 050	1	7.8	*
007-25-0804 North Atlantic Treaty Organization Security Investment Program					
Defense	Discretionary	Appropriation	250	7.8	20
Defense	Discretionary	Unobligated balance in 050	9	7.8	1
		Account Total	259		20
007-25-1205 Military Construction, Navy and Marine Corps					
Defense	Discretionary	Appropriation	2,100	7.8	164
Defense	Discretionary	Unobligated balance in 050	1,709	7.8	133
		Account Total	3,809		297
007-25-1235 Military Construction, Navy Reserve					
Defense	Discretionary	Appropriation	26	7.8	2
Defense	Discretionary	Unobligated balance in 050	39	7.8	3
		Account Total	65		5
007-25-2050 Military Construction, Army					
Defense	Discretionary	Appropriation	2,925	7.8	228
Defense	Discretionary	Unobligated balance in 050	2,300	7.8	179
		Account Total	5,225		408

* denotes $500,000 or less.

Sequestrable Budgetary Resources and Reductions in Sequestrable Resources by OMB Account -- FY 2013

(Amounts in millions)

Agency / Bureau / Account / Function / BEA Category / Budgetary Resource			Sequestrable BA Amount	Sequester Percentage	Sequester Amount
007-25-2085 Military Construction, Army National Guard					
Defense	Discretionary	Appropriation	803	7.8	63
Defense	Discretionary	Unobligated balance in 050	507	7.8	40
		Account Total	1,310		102
007-25-2086 Military Construction, Army Reserve					
Defense	Discretionary	Appropriation	282	7.8	22
Defense	Discretionary	Unobligated balance in 050	144	7.8	11
		Account Total	426		33
007-25-3300 Military Construction, Air Force					
Defense	Discretionary	Appropriation	1,202	7.8	94
Defense	Discretionary	Unobligated balance in 050	732	7.8	57
		Account Total	1,934		151
007-25-3730 Military Construction, Air Force Reserve					
Defense	Discretionary	Appropriation	34	7.8	3
Defense	Discretionary	Unobligated balance in 050	23	7.8	2
		Account Total	57		5
007-25-3830 Military Construction, Air National Guard					
Defense	Discretionary	Appropriation	117	7.8	9
Defense	Discretionary	Unobligated balance in 050	124	7.8	10
		Account Total	241		19
Family Housing					
007-30-0720 Family Housing Construction, Army					
Defense	Discretionary	Appropriation	178	7.8	14
Defense	Discretionary	Unobligated balance in 050	133	7.8	10
		Account Total	311		24
007-30-0725 Family Housing Operation and Maintenance, Army					
Defense	Discretionary	Appropriation	496	7.8	39
007-30-0730 Family Housing Construction, Navy and Marine Corps					
Defense	Discretionary	Appropriation	102	7.8	8
Defense	Discretionary	Unobligated balance in 050	245	7.8	19
		Account Total	347		27
007-30-0735 Family Housing Operation and Maintenance, Navy and Marine Corps					
Defense	Discretionary	Appropriation	370	7.8	29
007-30-0740 Family Housing Construction, Air Force					
Defense	Discretionary	Appropriation	60	7.8	5
Defense	Discretionary	Unobligated balance in 050	290	7.8	23
		Account Total	350		27
007-30-0745 Family Housing Operation and Maintenance, Air Force					
Defense	Discretionary	Appropriation	433	7.8	34
007-30-0765 Family Housing Operation and Maintenance, Defense-Wide					
Defense	Discretionary	Appropriation	51	7.8	4
007-30-0834 Department of Defense Family Housing Improvement Fund					
Defense	Discretionary	Appropriation	2	7.8	*
Defense	Discretionary	Unobligated balance in 050	118	7.8	9
		Account Total	120		9
007-30-4090 Homeowners Assistance Fund					
Defense	Discretionary	Appropriation	1	7.8	*
Defense	Discretionary	Unobligated balance in 050	245	7.8	19
		Account Total	246		19

Revolving and Management Funds

* denotes $500,000 or less.

Sequestrable Budgetary Resources and Reductions in Sequestrable Resources by OMB Account -- FY 2013

(Amounts in millions)

Agency / Bureau / Account / Function / BEA Category / Budgetary Resource	Sequestrable BA Amount	Sequester Percentage	Sequester Amount
007-40-4555 National Defense Stockpile Transaction Fund			
Defense Mandatory Spending authority	153	7.9	12
007-40-4557 National Defense Sealift Fund			
Defense Discretionary Appropriation	1,107	7.8	86
007-40-493001 Working Capital Fund, Army			
Defense Discretionary Appropriation	145	7.8	11
007-40-493002 Working Capital Fund, Navy			
Defense Discretionary Appropriation	24	7.8	2
007-40-493003 Working Capital Fund, Air Force			
Defense Discretionary Appropriation	305	7.8	24
007-40-493004 Working Capital Fund, Defense Commissary Agency			
Defense Discretionary Appropriation	1,385	7.8	108
007-40-493005 Working Capital Fund, Defense-Wide			
Defense Discretionary Appropriation	252	7.8	20
Trust Funds			
007-55-8164 Surcharge Collections, Sales of Commissary Stores, Defense			
Defense Mandatory Administrative expenses in otherwise exempt resources	251	7.9	20
007-55-9971 Other DOD Trust Funds			
Defense Mandatory Appropriation	26	7.9	2
Defense Mandatory Unobligated balance in 050	20	7.9	2
Account Total	46		4

Sequestrable Budgetary Resources and Reductions in Sequestrable Resources by OMB Account -- FY 2013

(Amounts in millions)

Agency / Bureau / Account / Function / BEA Category / Budgetary Resource	Sequestrable BA Amount	Sequester Percentage	Sequester Amount
Department of Education			
Office of Elementary and Secondary Education			
018-10-0101 Indian Student Education			
Nondefense Discretionary Appropriation	132	5.0	7
018-10-0102 Impact Aid			
Nondefense Discretionary Appropriation	1,299	5.0	65
018-10-0203 Supporting Student Success			
Nondefense Discretionary Appropriation	257	5.0	13
018-10-0900 Accelerating Achievement and Ensuring Equity			
Nondefense Discretionary Advance appropriation	10,841	5.0	542
Nondefense Discretionary Appropriation	4,931	5.0	247
Account Total	15,772		789
018-10-1000 Education Improvement Programs			
Nondefense Discretionary Advance appropriation	1,681	5.0	84
Nondefense Discretionary Appropriation	2,881	5.0	144
Account Total	4,562		228
Office of Innovation and Improvement			
018-12-0204 Innovation and Instructional Teams			
Nondefense Discretionary Appropriation	1,537	5.0	77
Office of English Language Acquisition			
018-15-1300 English Learner Education			
Nondefense Discretionary Appropriation	737	5.0	37
Office of Special Education and Rehabilitative Services			
018-20-0300 Special Education			
Nondefense Discretionary Advance appropriation	9,283	5.0	464
Nondefense Discretionary Appropriation	3,378	5.0	169
Account Total	12,661		633
018-20-0301 Rehabilitation Services and Disability Research			
Nondefense Discretionary Appropriation	392	5.0	20
Nondefense Mandatory Appropriation	3,231	5.1	165
Account Total	3,623		184
018-20-0600 American Printing House for the Blind			
Nondefense Discretionary Appropriation	25	5.0	1
018-20-0601 National Technical Institute for the Deaf			
Nondefense Discretionary Appropriation	66	5.0	3
018-20-0602 Gallaudet University			
Nondefense Discretionary Appropriation	126	5.0	6
Office of Vocational and Adult Education			
018-30-0400 Career, Technical and Adult Education			
Nondefense Discretionary Advance appropriation	791	5.0	40
Nondefense Discretionary Appropriation	952	5.0	48
Account Total	1,743		87
Office of Postsecondary Education			
018-40-0201 Higher Education			
Nondefense Discretionary Appropriation	1,881	5.0	94
Nondefense Mandatory Appropriation	428	5.1	22
Account Total	2,309		116

* denotes $500,000 or less.

Sequestrable Budgetary Resources and Reductions in Sequestrable Resources by OMB Account -- FY 2013

(Amounts in millions)

Agency / Bureau / Account / Function / BEA Category / Budgetary Resource			Sequestrable BA Amount	Sequester Percentage	Sequester Amount
018-40-0241 College Housing and Academic Facilities Loans Program Account					
Nondefense	Discretionary	Appropriation	21	5.0	1
018-40-0603 Howard University					
Nondefense	Discretionary	Appropriation	235	5.0	12
Office of Federal Student Aid					
018-45-0200 Student Financial Assistance					
Nondefense	Discretionary	Appropriation	1,722	5.0	86
Nondefense	Mandatory	Appropriation	*	5.1	*
		Account Total	1,722		86
018-45-0202 Student Aid Administration					
Nondefense	Discretionary	Appropriation	1,050	5.0	53
Nondefense	Mandatory	Appropriation	359	5.1	18
		Account Total	1,409		71
018-45-0206 Teacher Education Assistance					
Nondefense	Mandatory	Appropriation	23	5.1	1
018-45-5557 Student Financial Assistance Debt Collection					
Nondefense	Mandatory	Appropriation	10	5.1	1
Institute of Education Sciences					
018-50-1100 Institute of Education Sciences					
Nondefense	Discretionary	Appropriation	597	5.0	30
Departmental Management					
018-80-0700 Office for Civil Rights					
Nondefense	Discretionary	Appropriation	103	5.0	5
018-80-0800 Program Administration					
Nondefense	Discretionary	Appropriation	449	5.0	22
018-80-1400 Office of the Inspector General					
Nondefense	Discretionary	Appropriation	60	5.0	3

* denotes $500,000 or less.

Agency / Bureau / Account / Function / BEA Category / Budgetary Resource	Sequestrable BA Amount	Sequester Percentage	Sequester Amount
Department of Energy			
National Nuclear Security Administration			
019-05-0240 Weapons Activities			
Defense Discretionary Appropriation	7,557	7.8	589
Defense Discretionary Unobligated balance in 050	188	7.8	15
Account Total	7,745		604
019-05-0309 Defense Nuclear Nonproliferation			
Defense Discretionary Appropriation	2,410	7.8	188
Defense Discretionary Unobligated balance in 050	32	7.8	2
Account Total	2,442		191
019-05-0312 Cerro Grande Fire Activities			
Defense Discretionary Unobligated balance in 050	1	7.8	*
019-05-0313 Office of the Administrator			
Defense Discretionary Appropriation	413	7.8	32
Defense Discretionary Unobligated balance in 050	3	7.8	*
Account Total	416		32
019-05-0314 Naval Reactors			
Defense Discretionary Appropriation	1,087	7.8	85
Defense Discretionary Unobligated balance in 050	10	7.8	1
Account Total	1,097		86
Environmental and Other Defense Activities			
019-10-0243 Other Defense Activities			
Defense Discretionary Appropriation	828	7.8	65
Defense Discretionary Unobligated balance in 050	16	7.8	1
Account Total	844		66
019-10-0244 Defense Nuclear Waste Disposal			
Defense Discretionary Unobligated balance in 050	9	7.8	1
019-10-0251 Defense Environmental Cleanup			
Defense Discretionary Appropriation	5,034	7.8	393
Defense Discretionary Spending authority	1	7.8	*
Defense Discretionary Unobligated balance in 050	14	7.8	1
Account Total	5,049		394
Energy Programs			
019-20-0208 Title 17 Innovative Technology Loan Guarantee Program			
Nondefense Discretionary Spending authority	38	5.0	2
019-20-0212 Federal Energy Regulatory Commission			
Nondefense Discretionary Spending authority	306	5.0	15
019-20-0213 Fossil Energy Research and Development			
Nondefense Discretionary Appropriation	495	5.0	25
019-20-0216 Energy Information Administration			
Nondefense Discretionary Appropriation	106	5.0	5
019-20-0218 Strategic Petroleum Reserve			
Nondefense Discretionary Appropriation	194	5.0	10
019-20-0219 Naval Petroleum and Oil Shale Reserves			
Nondefense Discretionary Appropriation	15	5.0	1
019-20-0222 Science			
Nondefense Discretionary Appropriation	4,904	5.0	245

Sequestrable Budgetary Resources and Reductions in Sequestrable Resources by OMB Account -- FY 2013

(Amounts in millions)

Agency / Bureau / Account / Function / BEA Category / Budgetary Resource	Sequestrable BA Amount	Sequester Percentage	Sequester Amount
019-20-0315 Non-defense Environmental Cleanup			
Nondefense · Discretionary · Appropriation	237	5.0	12
019-20-0318 Electricity Delivery and Energy Reliability			
Defense · Discretionary · Appropriation	6	7.8	*
Nondefense · Discretionary · Appropriation	134	5.0	7
Account Total	140		7
019-20-0319 Nuclear Energy			
Nondefense · Discretionary · Appropriation	771	5.0	39
019-20-0321 Energy Efficiency and Renewable Energy			
Nondefense · Discretionary · Appropriation	1,821	5.0	91
019-20-0322 Advanced Technology Vehicles Manufacturing Loan Program Account			
Nondefense · Discretionary · Appropriation	6	5.0	*
019-20-0337 Advanced Research Projects Agency			
Nondefense · Discretionary · Appropriation	277	5.0	14
019-20-5105 Payments to States under Federal Power Act			
Nondefense · Mandatory · Appropriation	3	5.1	*
019-20-5231 Uranium Enrichment Decontamination and Decommissioning Fund			
Nondefense · Discretionary · Appropriation	475	5.0	24
019-20-5369 Northeast Home Heating Oil Reserve			
Nondefense · Discretionary · Appropriation	10	5.0	1
019-20-5523 Ultra-deepwater and Unconventional Natural Gas and Other Petroleum Research Fund			
Nondefense · Mandatory · Appropriation	50	5.1	3
Power Marketing Administration			
019-50-0303 Operation and Maintenance, Southwestern Power Administration			
Nondefense · Discretionary · Appropriation	13	5.0	1
019-50-4045 Bonneville Power Administration Fund			
Nondefense · Mandatory · Administrative expenses in otherwise exempt resources	115	5.1	6
019-50-4404 Western Area Power Administration, Borrowing Authority, Recovery Act.			
Nondefense · Mandatory · Borrowing authority	180	5.1	9
019-50-5068 Construction, Rehabilitation, Operation and Maintenance, Western Area Power Administration			
Nondefense · Discretionary · Appropriation	98	5.0	5
Departmental Administration			
019-60-0228 Departmental Administration			
Nondefense · Discretionary · Appropriation	131	5.0	7
019-60-0236 Office of the Inspector General			
Nondefense · Discretionary · Appropriation	42	5.0	2

* denotes $500,000 or less.

Sequestrable Budgetary Resources and Reductions in Sequestrable Resources by OMB Account -- FY 2013

(Amounts in millions)

Agency / Bureau / Account / Function / BEA Category / Budgetary Resource	Sequestrable BA Amount	Sequester Percentage	Sequester Amount
Department of Health and Human Services			
Food and Drug Administration			
009-10-4309 Revolving Fund for Certification and Other Services			
Nondefense　　Mandatory　　Spending authority	8	5.1	*
009-10-9911 Salaries and Expenses			
Nondefense　　Discretionary　　Appropriation	2,521	5.0	126
Nondefense　　Discretionary　　Spending authority	1,328	5.0	66
Nondefense　　Mandatory　　Spending authority	319	5.1	16
Account Total	4,168		209
Health Resources and Services Administration			
009-15-0321 Maternal, Infant, and Early Childhood Home Visiting Programs			
Nondefense　　Mandatory　　Appropriation	400	5.1	20
009-15-0340 Health Education Assistance Loans Program Account			
Nondefense　　Discretionary　　Appropriation	3	5.0	*
009-15-0350 Health Resources and Services			
Nondefense　　Discretionary　　Appropriation	6,232	5.0	312
Nondefense　　Discretionary　　Spending authority	11	5.0	1
Nondefense　　Mandatory　　Appropriation	498	5.1	25
Nondefense　　Mandatory　　Appropriation	1,352	2.0	27
Nondefense　　Mandatory　　Spending authority	16	5.1	1
Account Total	8,109		365
Indian Health Service			
009-17-0390 Indian Health Services			
Nondefense　　Discretionary　　Appropriation	3,890	5.0	195
Nondefense　　Mandatory　　Appropriation	150	2.0	3
Account Total	4,040		198
009-17-0391 Indian Health Facilities			
Nondefense　　Discretionary　　Appropriation	443	5.0	22
Centers for Disease Control and Prevention			
009-20-0943 CDC-Wide Activities and Program Support			
Nondefense　　Discretionary　　Appropriation	5,692	5.0	285
Nondefense　　Discretionary　　Spending authority	3	5.0	*
Defense　　Mandatory　　Appropriation	55	7.9	4
Defense　　Mandatory　　Unobligated balance in 050	2	7.9	*
Account Total	5,752		289
009-20-0944 Toxic Substances and Environmental Public Health, Agency for Toxic Substances and Disease Registry			
Nondefense　　Discretionary　　Appropriation	77	5.0	4
009-20-0946 World Trade Center Health Program Fund			
Nondefense　　Mandatory　　Appropriation	190	5.1	10
National Institutes of Health			
009-25-9915 National Institutes of Health			
Nondefense　　Discretionary　　Appropriation	30,899	5.0	1,545
Nondefense　　Mandatory　　Appropriation	150	5.1	8
Account Total	31,049		1,553
Substance Abuse and Mental Health Services Administration			
009-30-1362 Susbstance Abuse and Mental Health Services Administration			
Nondefense　　Discretionary　　Appropriation	3,368	5.0	168
Centers for Medicare and Medicaid Services			

* denotes $500,000 or less.

Sequestrable Budgetary Resources and Reductions in Sequestrable Resources by OMB Account -- FY 2013

(Amounts in millions)

Agency / Bureau / Account / Function / BEA Category / Budgetary Resource	Sequestrable BA Amount	Sequester Percentage	Sequester Amount
009-38-0115 Affordable Insurance Exchange Grants			
Nondefense Mandatory Appropriation	868	5.1	44
009-38-0511 Program Management			
Nondefense Discretionary Spending authority	458	5.0	23
Nondefense Mandatory Appropriation	253	5.1	13
Nondefense Mandatory Spending authority	72	5.1	4
Account Total	783		40
009-38-0516 State Grants and Demonstrations			
Nondefense Mandatory Appropriation	530	5.1	27
009-38-0524 Consumer Operated and Oriented Plan Program Contingency Fund			
Nondefense Mandatory Appropriation	253	5.1	13
009-38-8004 Federal Supplementary Medical Insurance Trust Fund			
Nondefense Discretionary Appropriation	3,446	5.0	172
Nondefense Mandatory Appropriation	128	5.1	7
Nondefense Mandatory Appropriation	257,533	2.0	5,151
Account Total	261,107		5,330
009-38-8005 Federal Hospital Insurance Trust Fund			
Nondefense Discretionary Appropriation	2,194	5.0	110
Nondefense Mandatory Appropriation	527	5.1	27
Nondefense Mandatory Appropriation	280,775	2.0	5,616
Account Total	283,496		5,752
009-38-8308 Medicare Prescription Drug Account, Federal Supplementary Insurance Trust Fund			
Nondefense Discretionary Appropriation	398	5.0	20
Nondefense Mandatory Appropriation	5	5.1	*
Nondefense Mandatory Appropriation	28,391	2.0	568
Account Total	28,794		588
009-38-8393 Health Care Fraud and Abuse Control Account			
Nondefense Discretionary Appropriation	312	5.0	16
Nondefense Mandatory Appropriation	484	5.1	25
Nondefense Mandatory Appropriation	812	2.0	16
Account Total	1,608		57
Administration for Children and Families			
009-70-1501 Payments to States for Child Support Enforcement and Family Support Programs			
Nondefense Mandatory Appropriation	1	5.1	*
009-70-1502 Low Income Home Energy Assistance			
Nondefense Discretionary Appropriation	3,493	5.0	175
009-70-1503 Refugee and Entrant Assistance			
Nondefense Discretionary Appropriation	900	5.0	45
009-70-1512 Supporting Healthy Families and Adolescent Development			
Nondefense Discretionary Appropriation	63	5.0	3
Nondefense Mandatory Appropriation	485	5.1	25
Account Total	548		28
009-70-1515 Payments to States for the Child Care and Development Block Grant			
Nondefense Discretionary Appropriation	2,292	5.0	115
009-70-1534 Social Services Block Grant			
Nondefense Mandatory Appropriation	2,285	5.1	117
009-70-1536 Children and Families Services Programs			
Nondefense Discretionary Appropriation	10,069	5.0	503

* denotes $500,000 or less.

Agency / Bureau / Account / Function / BEA Category / Budgetary Resource	Sequestrable BA Amount	Sequester Percentage	Sequester Amount
009-70-1545 Payments for Foster Care and Permanency			
Nondefense　　Mandatory　　Administrative expenses in otherwise exempt resources	*	5.1	*
009-70-1552 Temporary Assistance for Needy Families			
Nondefense　　Mandatory　　Administrative expenses in otherwise exempt resources	26	5.1	1
009-70-1553 Children's Research and Technical Assistance			
Nondefense　　Mandatory　　Administrative expenses in otherwise exempt resources	10	5.1	1
Nondefense　　Mandatory　　Appropriation	52	5.1	3
Nondefense　　Mandatory　　Spending authority	13	5.1	1
Account Total	75		4
Administration for Community Living			
009-75-0142 Aging and Disability Services Programs			
Nondefense　　Discretionary　　Appropriation	1,480	5.0	74
Nondefense　　Mandatory　　Appropriation	28	5.1	1
Account Total	1,508		75
Departmental Management			
009-90-0116 Prevention and Public Health Fund			
Nondefense　　Mandatory　　Appropriation	1,000	5.1	51
009-90-0117 Pregnancy Assistance Fund			
Nondefense　　Mandatory　　Appropriation	25	5.1	1
009-90-0130 Office of the National Coordinator for Health Information Technology			
Nondefense　　Discretionary　　Appropriation	17	5.0	1
009-90-0135 Office for Civil Rights			
Nondefense　　Discretionary　　Appropriation	41	5.0	2
Nondefense　　Discretionary　　Spending authority	6	5.0	*
Account Total	47		2
009-90-0140 Public Health and Social Services Emergency Fund			
Nondefense　　Discretionary　　Appropriation	767	5.0	38
009-90-9912 General Departmental Management			
Nondefense　　Discretionary　　Appropriation	477	5.0	24
Program Support Center			
009-91-0170 HHS Accrual Contribution to the Uniformed Services Retiree Health Care Fund			
Nondefense　　Discretionary　　Appropriation	29	5.0	1
009-91-9971 Miscellaneous Trust Funds			
Nondefense　　Mandatory　　Administrative expenses in otherwise exempt resources	45	5.1	2
Office of the Inspector General			
009-92-0128 Office of the Inspector General			
Nondefense　　Discretionary　　Appropriation	55	5.0	3
Nondefense　　Mandatory　　Spending authority	12	5.1	1
Account Total	67		3

* denotes $500,000 or less.

Sequestrable Budgetary Resources and Reductions in Sequestrable Resources by OMB Account -- FY 2013

(Amounts in millions)

Agency / Bureau / Account / Function / BEA Category / Budgetary Resource	Sequestrable BA Amount	Sequester Percentage	Sequester Amount
Department of Homeland Security			
Departmental Management and Operations			
024-10-0100 Departmental Operations			
Nondefense　　Discretionary　　Appropriation	479	5.0	24
024-10-0102 Office of the Chief Information Officer			
Nondefense　　Discretionary　　Appropriation	324	5.0	16
024-10-0115 Analysis and Operations			
Nondefense　　Discretionary　　Appropriation	340	5.0	17
Office of the Inspector General			
024-20-0200 Operating Expenses			
Nondefense　　Discretionary　　Appropriation	145	5.0	7
Citizenship and Immigration Services			
024-30-0300 Citizenship and Immigration Services			
Nondefense　　Discretionary　　Appropriation	103	5.0	5
Nondefense　　Mandatory　　Appropriation	2,859	5.1	146
Account Total	2,962		151
United States Secret Service			
024-40-0400 Operating Expenses			
Nondefense　　Discretionary　　Appropriation	1,670	5.0	84
024-40-0401 Acquisition, Construction, and Improvements			
Nondefense　　Discretionary　　Appropriation	5	5.0	*
Transportation Security Administration			
024-45-0541 Federal Air Marshals			
Nondefense　　Discretionary　　Appropriation	972	5.0	49
024-45-0550 Aviation Security			
Nondefense　　Discretionary　　Appropriation	3,178	5.0	159
Nondefense　　Discretionary　　Spending authority	2,094	5.0	105
Nondefense　　Mandatory　　Appropriation	250	5.1	13
Account Total	5,522		276
024-45-0551 Surface Transportation Security			
Nondefense　　Discretionary　　Appropriation	136	5.0	7
024-45-0554 Transportation Security Support			
Nondefense　　Discretionary　　Appropriation	1,038	5.0	52
024-45-0557 Transportation Threat Assessment and Credentialing			
Nondefense　　Discretionary　　Appropriation	165	5.0	8
Nondefense　　Discretionary　　Spending authority	75	5.0	4
Nondefense　　Mandatory　　Spending authority	5	5.1	*
Account Total	245		12
Federal Law Enforcement Training Center			
024-49-0509 Salaries and expenses			
Nondefense　　Discretionary　　Appropriation	240	5.0	12
Nondefense　　Discretionary　　Spending authority	2	5.0	*
Account Total	242		12
024-49-0510 Acquisitions, Construction, Improvements and Related Expenses			
Nondefense　　Discretionary　　Appropriation	32	5.0	2
Immigration and Customs Enforcement			

Sequestrable Budgetary Resources and Reductions in Sequestrable Resources by OMB Account -- FY 2013

(Amounts in millions)

Agency / Bureau / Account / Function / BEA Category / Budgetary Resource	Sequestrable BA Amount	Sequester Percentage	Sequester Amount
024-55-0540 Immigration and Customs Enforcement			
Nondefense Discretionary Appropriation	5,554	5.0	278
Nondefense Mandatory Appropriation	312	5.1	16
Account Total	5,866		294
024-55-0543 Automation Modernization, Immigration and Customs Enforcement			
Nondefense Discretionary Appropriation	12	5.0	1
Customs and Border Protection			
024-58-0530 Customs and Border Protection			
Nondefense Discretionary Appropriation	8,737	5.0	437
Nondefense Mandatory Appropriation	1,464	5.1	75
Account Total	10,201		512
024-58-0531 Automation Modernization, Customs and Border Protection			
Nondefense Discretionary Appropriation	331	5.0	17
024-58-0532 Construction, Customs and Border Protection			
Nondefense Discretionary Appropriation	238	5.0	12
024-58-0533 Border Security Fencing, Infrastructure, and Technology			
Nondefense Discretionary Appropriation	399	5.0	20
024-58-0544 Air and Marine Interdiction, Operations, Maintenance, and Procurement			
Nondefense Discretionary Appropriation	507	5.0	25
024-58-5533 Payments to Wool Manufacturers			
Nondefense Mandatory Appropriation	15	5.1	1
024-58-5543 International Registered Traveler			
Nondefense Discretionary Appropriation	14	5.0	1
024-58-5595 Electronic System for Travel Authorization			
Nondefense Mandatory Appropriation	46	5.1	2
024-58-5687 Refunds, Transfers, and Expenses of Operation, Puerto Rico			
Nondefense Mandatory Appropriation	96	5.1	5
024-58-8789 US Customs Refunds, Transfers and Expenses, Unclaimed and Abandoned Goods			
Nondefense Mandatory Appropriation	4	5.1	*
United States Coast Guard			
024-60-0610 Operating Expenses			
Defense Discretionary Appropriation	532	7.8	41
Nondefense Discretionary Appropriation	3,044	5.0	152
Account Total	3,576		194
024-60-0611 Environmental Compliance and Restoration			
Nondefense Discretionary Appropriation	14	5.0	1
024-60-0612 Reserve Training			
Nondefense Discretionary Appropriation	36	5.0	2
024-60-0613 Acquisition, Construction, and Improvements			
Nondefense Discretionary Appropriation	1,681	5.0	84
024-60-0615 Research, Development, Test, and Evaluation			
Nondefense Discretionary Appropriation	26	5.0	1
024-60-8149 Boat Safety			
Nondefense Mandatory Appropriation	116	5.1	6
024-60-8314 Trust Fund Share of Expenses			
Nondefense Discretionary Appropriation	45	5.0	2

* denotes $500,000 or less.

Agency / Bureau / Account / Function / BEA Category / Budgetary Resource	Sequestrable BA Amount	Sequester Percentage	Sequester Amount
024-60-8349 Maritime Oil Spill Programs			
Nondefense · Mandatory · Appropriation	101	5.1	5
National Protection and Programs Directorate			
024-65-0117 Office of Health Affairs			
Nondefense · Discretionary · Appropriation	168	5.0	8
024-65-0521 United States Visitor and Immigrant Status Indicator Technology			
Nondefense · Discretionary · Appropriation	282	5.0	14
024-65-0565 Infrastructure Protection and Information Security			
Defense · Discretionary · Appropriation	1,170	7.8	91
Defense · Discretionary · Unobligated balance in 050	1	7.8	*
Account Total	1,171		91
024-65-0566 National Protection and Programs Directorate			
Nondefense · Discretionary · Appropriation	50	5.0	3
Federal Emergency Management Agency			
024-70-0500 Flood Hazard Mapping and Risk Analysis Program			
Nondefense · Discretionary · Appropriation	99	5.0	5
024-70-0560 State and Local Programs			
Defense · Discretionary · Appropriation	50	7.8	4
Nondefense · Discretionary · Appropriation	2,251	5.0	113
Account Total	2,301		117
024-70-0564 United States Fire Administration and Training			
Nondefense · Discretionary · Appropriation	44	5.0	2
024-70-0700 Salaries and Expenses			
Defense · Discretionary · Appropriation	75	7.8	6
Nondefense · Discretionary · Appropriation	917	5.0	46
Account Total	992		52
024-70-0702 Disaster Relief			
Nondefense · Discretionary · Appropriation	18,565	5.0	928
024-70-0703 Disaster Assistance Direct Loan Program Account			
Nondefense · Discretionary · Appropriation	300	5.0	15
024-70-0707 Emergency Food and Shelter			
Nondefense · Discretionary · Appropriation	121	5.0	6
024-70-0715 Radiological Emergency Preparedness Program			
Nondefense · Discretionary · Spending authority	38	5.0	2
024-70-0716 National Pre-disaster Mitigation Fund			
Nondefense · Discretionary · Appropriation	36	5.0	2
024-70-4236 National Flood Insurance Fund			
Nondefense · Mandatory · Administrative expenses in otherwise exempt resources	66	5.1	3
Science and Technology			
024-80-0800 Research, Development, Acquisitions and Operations			
Nondefense · Discretionary · Appropriation	675	5.0	34
Domestic Nuclear Detection Office			
024-85-0860 Research, Development, and Operations			
Nondefense · Discretionary · Appropriation	216	5.0	11
024-85-0861 Management and Administration			
Nondefense · Discretionary · Appropriation	38	5.0	2

* denotes $500,000 or less.

Sequestrable Budgetary Resources and Reductions in Sequestrable Resources by OMB Account -- FY 2013

(Amounts in millions)

Agency / Bureau / Account / Function / BEA Category / Budgetary Resource	Sequestrable BA Amount	Sequester Percentage	Sequester Amount
024-85-0862 Systems Acquisition			
Nondefense Discretionary Appropriation	41	5.0	2

Agency / Bureau / Account / Function / BEA Category / Budgetary Resource	Sequestrable BA Amount	Sequester Percentage	Sequester Amount
Department of Housing and Urban Development			
Public and Indian Housing Programs			
025-03-0163 Public Housing Operating Fund			
Nondefense Discretionary Appropriation	3,986	5.0	199
025-03-0223 Indian Housing Loan Guarantee Fund Program Account			
Nondefense Discretionary Appropriation	6	5.0	*
025-03-0235 Native Hawaiian Housing Block Grant			
Nondefense Discretionary Appropriation	13	5.0	1
025-03-0302 Tenant Based Rental Assistance			
Nondefense Discretionary Advance appropriation	4,000	5.0	200
Nondefense Discretionary Appropriation	14,753	5.0	738
Account Total	18,753		938
025-03-0303 Project-based Rental Assistance			
Nondefense Discretionary Advance appropriation	400	5.0	20
Nondefense Discretionary Appropriation	8,995	5.0	450
Account Total	9,395		470
025-03-0304 Public Housing Capital Fund			
Nondefense Discretionary Appropriation	1,886	5.0	94
025-03-0313 Native American Housing Block Grant			
Nondefense Discretionary Appropriation	654	5.0	33
025-03-0349 Choice Neighborhoods			
Nondefense Discretionary Appropriation	121	5.0	6
Community Planning and Development			
025-06-0162 Community Development Fund			
Nondefense Discretionary Appropriation	19,308	5.0	965
025-06-0176 Self-help Homeownership Opportunity Program			
Nondefense Discretionary Appropriation	54	5.0	3
025-06-0192 Homeless Assistance Grants			
Nondefense Discretionary Appropriation	1,913	5.0	96
025-06-0198 Community Development Loan Guarantees Program Account			
Nondefense Discretionary Appropriation	6	5.0	*
025-06-0205 Home Investment Partnership Program			
Nondefense Discretionary Appropriation	1,006	5.0	50
025-06-0308 Housing Opportunities for Persons with AIDS			
Nondefense Discretionary Appropriation	334	5.0	17
Housing Programs			
025-09-0156 Housing Counseling Assistance			
Nondefense Discretionary Appropriation	45	5.0	2
025-09-0183 FHA-mutual Mortgage Insurance Program Account			
Nondefense Discretionary Appropriation	208	5.0	10
025-09-0237 Housing for Persons with Disabilities			
Nondefense Discretionary Appropriation	166	5.0	8
025-09-0320 Housing for the Elderly			
Nondefense Discretionary Appropriation	377	5.0	19

Sequestrable Budgetary Resources and Reductions in Sequestrable Resources by OMB Account -- FY 2013

(Amounts in millions)

Agency / Bureau / Account / Function / BEA Category / Budgetary Resource	Sequestrable BA Amount	Sequester Percentage	Sequester Amount
025-09-4041 Rental Housing Assistance Fund			
Nondefense — Mandatory — Spending authority	3	5.1	*
025-09-4044 Flexible Subsidy Fund			
Nondefense — Discretionary — Spending authority	21	5.0	1
025-09-8119 Manufactured Housing Fees Trust Fund			
Nondefense — Discretionary — Appropriation	7	5.0	*
Government National Mortgage Association			
025-12-0186 Guarantees of Mortgage-backed Securities Loan Guarantee Program Account			
Nondefense — Discretionary — Spending authority	20	5.0	1
Policy Development and Research			
025-28-0108 Research and Technology			
Nondefense — Discretionary — Appropriation	46	5.0	2
Fair Housing and Equal Opportunity			
025-29-0144 Fair Housing Activities			
Nondefense — Discretionary — Appropriation	71	5.0	4
Office of Lead Hazard Control and Healthy Homes			
025-32-0174 Lead Hazard Reduction			
Nondefense — Discretionary — Appropriation	121	5.0	6
Management and Administration			
025-35-0189 Office of Inspector General			
Nondefense — Discretionary — Appropriation	135	5.0	7
025-35-0334 Housing Personnel Compensation and Benefits			
Nondefense — Discretionary — Appropriation	394	5.0	20
025-35-0335 Administrative Support Offices			
Nondefense — Discretionary — Appropriation	541	5.0	27
025-35-0337 Public and Indian Housing Personnel Compensation and Benefits			
Nondefense — Discretionary — Appropriation	201	5.0	10
025-35-0338 Community Planning and Development Personnel Compensation and Benefits			
Nondefense — Discretionary — Appropriation	111	5.0	6
025-35-0339 Policy Development and Research Personnel Compensation and Benefits			
Nondefense — Discretionary — Appropriation	22	5.0	1
025-35-0340 Fair Housing and Equal Opportunity Personnel Compensation and Benefits			
Nondefense — Discretionary — Appropriation	73	5.0	4
025-35-0341 Office of Healthy Homes and Lead Hazard Control Personnel Compensation and Benefits			
Nondefense — Discretionary — Appropriation	7	5.0	*
025-35-0402 Transformation Initiative			
Nondefense — Discretionary — Appropriation	50	5.0	3
025-35-4586 Information Technology Portfolio			
Nondefense — Discretionary — Appropriation	200	5.0	10

* denotes $500,000 or less.

Sequestrable Budgetary Resources and Reductions in Sequestrable Resources by OMB Account -- FY 2013

(Amounts in millions)

Agency / Bureau / Account / Function / BEA Category / Budgetary Resource	Sequestrable BA Amount	Sequester Percentage	Sequester Amount
Department of the Interior			
Bureau of Land Management			
010-04-1109 Management of Lands and Resources			
Nondefense Discretionary Appropriation	966	5.0	48
Nondefense Discretionary Spending authority	75	5.0	4
Account Total	1,041		52
010-04-1110 Construction			
Nondefense Discretionary Appropriation	4	5.0	*
010-04-1116 Oregon and California Grant Lands			
Nondefense Discretionary Appropriation	113	5.0	6
010-04-4053 Helium Fund			
Nondefense Mandatory Administrative expenses in otherwise exempt resources	16	5.1	1
010-04-4525 Working Capital Fund			
Nondefense Discretionary Spending authority	9	5.0	*
010-04-5017 Service Charges, Deposits, and Forfeitures			
Nondefense Discretionary Appropriation	31	5.0	2
010-04-5033 Land Acquisition			
Nondefense Discretionary Appropriation	22	5.0	1
010-04-5132 Range Improvements			
Nondefense Mandatory Appropriation	10	5.1	1
010-04-9921 Miscellaneous Permanent Payment Accounts			
Nondefense Mandatory Appropriation	62	5.1	3
010-04-9926 Permanent Operating Funds			
Nondefense Mandatory Administrative expenses in otherwise exempt resources	16	5.1	1
Nondefense Mandatory Appropriation	131	5.1	7
Account Total	147		8
010-04-9971 Miscellaneous Trust Funds			
Nondefense Mandatory Administrative expenses in otherwise exempt resources	21	5.1	1
Bureau of Ocean Energy Management			
010-06-1917 Ocean Energy Management			
Nondefense Discretionary Appropriation	60	5.0	3
Nondefense Discretionary Spending authority	101	5.0	5
Account Total	161		8
Office of Surface Mining Reclamation and Enforcement			
010-08-1801 Regulation and Technology			
Nondefense Discretionary Appropriation	124	5.0	6
Nondefense Discretionary Spending authority	3	5.0	*
Account Total	127		6
010-08-1803 Payments to States in Lieu of Coal Fee Receipts			
Nondefense Mandatory Appropriation	128	5.1	7
010-08-5015 Abandoned Mine Reclamation Fund			
Nondefense Discretionary Appropriation	28	5.0	1
Nondefense Mandatory Appropriation	221	5.1	11
Account Total	249		13
Bureau of Reclamation			

Sequestrable Budgetary Resources and Reductions in Sequestrable Resources by OMB Account -- FY 2013

(Amounts in millions)

Agency / Bureau / Account / Function / BEA Category / Budgetary Resource			Sequestrable BA Amount	Sequester Percentage	Sequester Amount
010-10-0680 Water and Related Resources					
Nondefense	Discretionary	Appropriation	883	5.0	44
Nondefense	Discretionary	Spending authority	212	5.0	11
Nondefense	Mandatory	Appropriation	1	5.1	*
		Account Total	1,096		55
010-10-0687 California Bay-Delta Restoration					
Nondefense	Discretionary	Appropriation	40	5.0	2
010-10-4079 Lower Colorado River Basin Development Fund					
Nondefense	Discretionary	Appropriation	6	5.0	*
Nondefense	Mandatory	Administrative expenses in otherwise exempt resources	247	5.1	13
Nondefense	Mandatory	Spending authority	1	5.1	*
		Account Total	254		13
010-10-4081 Upper Colorado River Basin Fund					
Nondefense	Discretionary	Appropriation	11	5.0	1
Nondefense	Mandatory	Administrative expenses in otherwise exempt resources	81	5.1	4
		Account Total	92		5
010-10-4524 Working Capital Fund					
Nondefense	Discretionary	Spending authority	13	5.0	1
010-10-5065 Policy and Administration					
Nondefense	Discretionary	Appropriation	60	5.0	3
010-10-5173 Central Valley Project Restoration Fund					
Nondefense	Discretionary	Appropriation	53	5.0	3
010-10-5656 Colorado River Dam Fund, Boulder Canyon Project					
Nondefense	Mandatory	Administrative expenses in otherwise exempt resources	16	5.1	1
010-10-8070 Reclamation Trust Funds					
Nondefense	Mandatory	Administrative expenses in otherwise exempt resources	2	5.1	*
Central Utah Project					
010-11-0787 Central Utah Project Completion Account					
Nondefense	Discretionary	Appropriation	27	5.0	1
010-11-5174 Utah Reclamation Mitigation and Conservation Account					
Nondefense	Discretionary	Appropriation	2	5.0	*
United States Geological Survey					
010-12-0804 Surveys, Investigations, and Research					
Nondefense	Discretionary	Appropriation	1,075	5.0	54
United States Fish and Wildlife Service					
010-18-1611 Resource Management					
Nondefense	Discretionary	Appropriation	1,234	5.0	62
Nondefense	Discretionary	Spending authority	55	5.0	3
		Account Total	1,289		64
010-18-1612 Construction					
Nondefense	Discretionary	Appropriation	91	5.0	5
010-18-1652 Multinational Species Conservation Fund					
Nondefense	Discretionary	Appropriation	10	5.0	1
010-18-1696 Neotropical Migratory Bird Conservation					
Nondefense	Discretionary	Appropriation	4	5.0	*
010-18-5020 Land Acquisition					
Nondefense	Discretionary	Appropriation	55	5.0	3

* denotes $500,000 or less.

Agency / Bureau / Account / Function / BEA Category / Budgetary Resource	Sequestrable BA Amount	Sequester Percentage	Sequester Amount
010-18-5029 Federal Aid in Wildlife Restoration			
Nondefense Mandatory Appropriation	413	5.1	21
010-18-5091 National Wildlife Refuge Fund			
Nondefense Discretionary Appropriation	14	5.0	1
Nondefense Mandatory Appropriation	8	5.1	*
Account Total	22		1
010-18-5137 Migratory Bird Conservation Account			
Nondefense Mandatory Appropriation	47	5.1	2
010-18-5143 Cooperative Endangered Species Conservation Fund			
Nondefense Discretionary Appropriation	48	5.0	2
010-18-5241 North American Wetlands Conservation Fund			
Nondefense Discretionary Appropriation	36	5.0	2
Nondefense Mandatory Appropriation	1	5.1	*
Account Total	37		2
010-18-5252 Recreation Enhancement Fee Program, FWS			
Nondefense Mandatory Administrative expenses in otherwise exempt resources	1	5.1	*
010-18-5474 State Wildlife Grants			
Nondefense Discretionary Appropriation	62	5.0	3
010-18-8151 Sport Fish Restoration			
Nondefense Mandatory Appropriation	446	5.1	23
Bureau of Safety and Environmental Enforcement			
010-22-1700 Offshore Safety and Environmental Enforcement			
Nondefense Discretionary Appropriation	62	5.0	3
Nondefense Discretionary Spending authority	121	5.0	6
Account Total	183		9
010-22-1920 Oil Spill Research			
Nondefense Discretionary Appropriation	3	5.0	*
010-22-8370 Oil Spill Research			
Nondefense Discretionary Appropriation	15	5.0	1
National Park Service			
010-24-1036 Operation of the National Park System			
Nondefense Discretionary Appropriation	2,250	5.0	113
010-24-1039 Construction (and Major Maintenance)			
Nondefense Discretionary Appropriation	505	5.0	25
010-24-1042 National Recreation and Preservation			
Nondefense Discretionary Appropriation	60	5.0	3
010-24-5035 Land Acquisition and State Assistance			
Nondefense Discretionary Appropriation	103	5.0	5
010-24-5140 Historic Preservation Fund			
Nondefense Discretionary Appropriation	106	5.0	5
010-24-9924 Other Permanent Appropriations			
Nondefense Mandatory Administrative expenses in otherwise exempt resources	8	5.1	*
010-24-9928 Recreation Fee Permanent Appropriations			
Nondefense Mandatory Administrative expenses in otherwise exempt resources	34	5.1	2
Nondefense Mandatory Appropriation	1	5.1	*
Account Total	35		2
Bureau of Indian Affairs and Bureau of Indian Education			

Sequestrable Budgetary Resources and Reductions in Sequestrable Resources by OMB Account -- FY 2013

(Amounts in millions)

Agency / Bureau / Account / Function / BEA Category / Budgetary Resource	Sequestrable BA Amount	Sequester Percentage	Sequester Amount
010-76-2100 Operation of Indian Programs			
Nondefense Discretionary Appropriation	2,382	5.0	119
010-76-2301 Construction			
Nondefense Discretionary Appropriation	124	5.0	6
010-76-2628 Indian Guaranteed Loan Program Account			
Nondefense Discretionary Appropriation	7	5.0	*
010-76-5051 Operation and Maintenance of Quarters			
Nondefense Mandatory Administrative expenses in otherwise exempt resources	3	5.1	*
010-76-9925 Miscellaneous Permanent Appropriations			
Nondefense Mandatory Administrative expenses in otherwise exempt resources	19	5.1	1
Departmental Offices			
010-84-0102 Salaries and Expenses			
Nondefense Discretionary Appropriation	624	5.0	31
010-84-5003 Mineral Leasing and Associated Payments			
Nondefense Mandatory Appropriation	2,144	5.1	109
010-84-5045 National Petroleum Reserve, Alaska			
Nondefense Mandatory Appropriation	3	5.1	*
010-84-5243 National Forests Fund, Payment to States			
Nondefense Mandatory Appropriation	9	5.1	*
010-84-5248 Leases of Lands Acquired for Flood Control, Navigation, and Allied Purposes			
Nondefense Mandatory Appropriation	19	5.1	1
010-84-5574 Geothermal Lease Revenues, Payment to Counties			
Nondefense Mandatory Appropriation	4	5.1	*
Insular Affairs			
010-85-0412 Assistance to Territories			
Nondefense Mandatory Administrative expenses in otherwise exempt resources	10	5.1	1
Office of the Solicitor			
010-86-0107 Salaries and Expenses			
Nondefense Discretionary Appropriation	67	5.0	3
Office of Inspector General			
010-88-0104 Salaries and Expenses			
Nondefense Discretionary Appropriation	50	5.0	3
Office of the Special Trustee for American Indians			
010-90-0120 Federal Trust Programs			
Nondefense Discretionary Appropriation	153	5.0	8
National Indian Gaming Commission			
010-92-0118 Salaries and Expenses			
Nondefense Discretionary Spending authority	3	5.0	*
010-92-5141 National Indian Gaming Commission, Gaming Activity Fees			
Nondefense Mandatory Appropriation	18	5.1	1
Department-Wide Programs			
010-95-1114 Payments in Lieu of Taxes			
Nondefense Mandatory Appropriation	398	5.1	20
010-95-1121 Central Hazardous Materials Fund			
Nondefense Discretionary Appropriation	10	5.0	1

* denotes $500,000 or less.

Sequestrable Budgetary Resources and Reductions in Sequestrable Resources by OMB Account -- FY 2013

(Amounts in millions)

Agency / Bureau / Account / Function / BEA Category / Budgetary Resource			Sequestrable BA Amount	Sequester Percentage	Sequester Amount
010-95-1125 Wildland Fire Management					
Nondefense	Discretionary	Appropriation	750	5.0	38
010-95-1618 Natural Resource Damage Assessment Fund					
Nondefense	Mandatory	Administrative expenses in otherwise exempt resources	4	5.1	*
010-95-4523 Working Capital Fund					
Nondefense	Discretionary	Appropriation	62	5.0	3
Nondefense	Discretionary	Spending authority	12	5.0	1
		Account Total	74		4

Agency / Bureau / Account / Function / BEA Category / Budgetary Resource	Sequestrable BA Amount	Sequester Percentage	Sequester Amount
Department of Justice			
General Administration			
011-03-0129 Salaries and Expenses			
Nondefense Discretionary Appropriation	112	5.0	6
011-03-0132 Tactical Law Enforcement Wireless Communications			
Nondefense Discretionary Appropriation	88	5.0	4
011-03-0134 Justice Information Sharing Technology			
Nondefense Discretionary Appropriation	44	5.0	2
011-03-0136 Detention Trustee			
Nondefense Discretionary Appropriation	1,590	5.0	80
011-03-0328 Office of Inspector General			
Nondefense Discretionary Appropriation	85	5.0	4
011-03-0339 Administrative Review and Appeals			
Nondefense Discretionary Appropriation	307	5.0	15
011-03-1102 National Drug Intelligence Center			
Nondefense Discretionary Appropriation	20	5.0	1
United States Parole Commission			
011-04-1061 Salaries and Expenses			
Nondefense Discretionary Appropriation	13	5.0	1
Legal Activities and U.S. Marshals			
011-05-0100 Salaries and Expenses, Foreign Claims Settlement Commission			
Nondefense Discretionary Appropriation	2	5.0	*
011-05-0128 Salaries and Expenses, General Legal Activities			
Nondefense Discretionary Appropriation	868	5.0	43
011-05-0133 Construction			
Nondefense Discretionary Appropriation	15	5.0	1
011-05-0311 Fees and Expenses of Witnesses			
Nondefense Mandatory Appropriation	270	5.1	14
011-05-0319 Salaries and Expenses, Antitrust Division			
Nondefense Discretionary Appropriation	43	5.0	2
011-05-0322 Salaries and Expenses, United States Attorneys			
Nondefense Discretionary Appropriation	1,972	5.0	99
011-05-0324 Salaries and Expenses, United States Marshals Service			
Nondefense Discretionary Appropriation	1,179	5.0	59
011-05-0340 September 11th Victim Compensation (general Fund)			
Nondefense Mandatory Appropriation	322	5.1	16
011-05-0500 Salaries and Expenses, Community Relations Service			
Nondefense Discretionary Appropriation	11	5.0	1
011-05-5042 Assets Forfeiture Fund			
Nondefense Discretionary Appropriation	21	5.0	1
Nondefense Mandatory Appropriation	1,358	5.1	69
Account Total	1,379		70
011-05-5073 United States Trustee System Fund			
Nondefense Discretionary Appropriation	224	5.0	11
Interagency Law Enforcement			

Sequestrable Budgetary Resources and Reductions in Sequestrable Resources by OMB Account -- FY 2013

(Amounts in millions)

Agency / Bureau / Account / Function / BEA Category / Budgetary Resource			Sequestrable BA Amount	Sequester Percentage	Sequester Amount
011-07-0323 Interagency Crime and Drug Enforcement					
Nondefense	Discretionary	Appropriation	531	5.0	27
National Security Division					
011-08-1300 Salaries and Expenses					
Nondefense	Discretionary	Appropriation	88	5.0	4
Federal Bureau of Investigation					
011-10-0200 Salaries and Expenses					
Defense	Discretionary	Appropriation	4,775	7.8	372
Defense	Discretionary	Unobligated balance in 050	169	7.8	13
Nondefense	Discretionary	Appropriation	3,321	5.0	166
		Account Total	8,265		552
011-10-0203 Construction					
Nondefense	Discretionary	Appropriation	81	5.0	4
Drug Enforcement Administration					
011-12-1100 Salaries and Expenses					
Nondefense	Discretionary	Appropriation	2,041	5.0	102
011-12-1101 Construction					
Nondefense	Discretionary	Appropriation	10	5.0	1
011-12-5131 Diversion Control Fee Account					
Nondefense	Mandatory	Appropriation	335	5.1	17
Bureau of Alcohol, Tobacco, Firearms, and Explosives					
011-14-0700 Salaries and Expenses					
Nondefense	Discretionary	Appropriation	1,159	5.0	58
Federal Prison System					
011-20-1003 Buildings and Facilities					
Nondefense	Discretionary	Appropriation	55	5.0	3
011-20-1060 Salaries and Expenses					
Nondefense	Discretionary	Appropriation	6,591	5.0	330
011-20-8408 Commissary Funds, Federal Prisons (trust Revolving Fund)					
Nondefense	Mandatory	Administrative expenses in otherwise exempt resources	111	5.1	6
Office of Justice Programs					
011-21-0401 Research, Evaluation, and Statistics					
Nondefense	Discretionary	Appropriation	105	5.0	5
011-21-0404 State and Local Law Enforcement Assistance					
Nondefense	Discretionary	Appropriation	1,126	5.0	56
011-21-0405 Juvenile Justice Programs					
Nondefense	Discretionary	Appropriation	255	5.0	13
011-21-0406 Community Oriented Policing Services					
Nondefense	Discretionary	Appropriation	163	5.0	8
011-21-0409 Violence against Women Prevention and Prosecution Programs					
Nondefense	Discretionary	Appropriation	400	5.0	20
011-21-5041 Crime Victims Fund					
Nondefense	Mandatory	Appropriation	705	5.1	36

Sequestrable Budgetary Resources and Reductions in Sequestrable Resources by OMB Account -- FY 2013

(Amounts in millions)

Agency / Bureau / Account / Function / BEA Category / Budgetary Resource	Sequestrable BA Amount	Sequester Percentage	Sequester Amount
Department of Labor			
Employment and Training Administration			
012-05-0168 Short Time Compensation Programs			
Nondefense Mandatory Appropriation	219	5.1	11
012-05-0172 Program Administration			
Nondefense Discretionary Appropriation	98	5.0	5
012-05-0174 Training and Employment Services			
Nondefense Discretionary Advance appropriation	1,772	5.0	89
Nondefense Discretionary Appropriation	1,454	5.0	73
Nondefense Mandatory Appropriation	125	5.1	6
Account Total	3,351		168
012-05-0175 Community Service Employment for Older Americans			
Nondefense Discretionary Appropriation	451	5.0	23
012-05-0179 State Unemployment Insurance and Employment Service Operations			
Nondefense Discretionary Appropriation	88	5.0	4
Nondefense Mandatory Appropriation	13	5.1	1
Account Total	101		5
012-05-0181 Office of Job Corps			
Nondefense Discretionary Appropriation	1,713	5.0	86
012-05-0187 TAA Community College and Career Training Grant Fund			
Nondefense Mandatory Appropriation	500	5.1	26
012-05-0326 Federal Unemployment Benefits and Allowances			
Nondefense Mandatory Appropriation	1,132	5.1	58
012-05-8042 Unemployment Trust Fund			
Nondefense Discretionary Appropriation	4,363	5.0	218
Nondefense Mandatory Administrative expenses in otherwise exempt resources	92	5.1	5
Nondefense Mandatory Appropriation	46,851	5.1	2,389
Account Total	51,306		2,612
Employee Benefits Security Administration			
012-11-1700 Salaries and Expenses			
Nondefense Discretionary Appropriation	184	5.0	9
Pension Benefit Guaranty Corporation			
012-12-4204 Pension Benefit Guaranty Corporation Fund			
Nondefense Mandatory Administrative expenses in otherwise exempt resources	118	5.1	6
Office of Workers' Compensation Programs			
012-15-0163 Salaries and Expenses			
Nondefense Discretionary Appropriation	117	5.0	6
012-15-0169 Special Benefits for Disabled Coal Miners			
Nondefense Mandatory Administrative expenses in otherwise exempt resources	5	5.1	*
012-15-1524 Administrative Expenses, Energy Employees Occupational Illness Compensation Fund			
Defense Mandatory Appropriation	129	7.9	10
Defense Mandatory Unobligated balance in 050	2	7.9	*
Account Total	131		10
012-15-8144 Black Lung Disability Trust Fund			
Nondefense Mandatory Administrative expenses in otherwise exempt resources	59	5.1	3
012-15-9971 Special Workers' Compensation Expenses			
Nondefense Mandatory Administrative expenses in otherwise exempt resources	2	5.1	*

* denotes $500,000 or less.

Agency / Bureau / Account / Function / BEA Category / Budgetary Resource			Sequestrable BA Amount	Sequester Percentage	Sequester Amount
Wage and Hour Division					
012-16-0143 Salaries and Expenses					
Nondefense	Discretionary	Appropriation	228	5.0	11
Nondefense	Discretionary	Spending authority	3	5.0	*
		Account Total	231		12
012-16-5393 H-1 B and L Fraud Prevention and Detection					
Nondefense	Mandatory	Appropriation	35	5.1	2
Occupational Safety and Health Administration					
012-18-0400 Salaries and Expenses					
Nondefense	Discretionary	Appropriation	568	5.0	28
Mine Safety and Health Administration					
012-19-1200 Salaries and Expenses					
Nondefense	Discretionary	Appropriation	376	5.0	19
Nondefense	Discretionary	Spending authority	1	5.0	*
		Account Total	377		19
Bureau of Labor Statistics					
012-20-0200 Salaries and Expenses					
Nondefense	Discretionary	Appropriation	545	5.0	27
Office of Federal Contract Compliance Programs					
012-22-0148 Salaries and Expenses					
Nondefense	Discretionary	Appropriation	106	5.0	5
Office of Labor Management Standards					
012-23-0150 Salaries and Expenses					
Nondefense	Discretionary	Appropriation	41	5.0	2
Departmental Management					
012-25-0106 Office of the Inspector General					
Nondefense	Discretionary	Appropriation	78	5.0	4
012-25-0162 Information Technology Modernization					
Nondefense	Discretionary	Appropriation	20	5.0	1
012-25-0164 Veterans Employment and Training					
Nondefense	Discretionary	Appropriation	53	5.0	3
012-25-0165 Salaries and Expenses					
Nondefense	Discretionary	Appropriation	348	5.0	17
012-25-0166 Office of Disability Employment Policy					
Nondefense	Discretionary	Appropriation	39	5.0	2

(Amounts in millions)

Agency / Bureau / Account / Function / BEA Category / Budgetary Resource	Sequestrable BA Amount	Sequester Percentage	Sequester Amount
Department of State			
Administration of Foreign Affairs			
014-05-0113 Diplomatic and Consular Programs			
Nondefense Discretionary Appropriation	10,966	5.0	548
Nondefense Discretionary Spending authority	2,290	5.0	115
Nondefense Mandatory Appropriation	35	5.1	2
Account Total	13,291		665
014-05-0120 Capital Investment Fund			
Nondefense Discretionary Appropriation	60	5.0	3
014-05-0121 Conflict Stabilization Operations			
Nondefense Discretionary Appropriation	8	5.0	*
014-05-0209 Educational and Cultural Exchange Programs			
Nondefense Discretionary Appropriation	602	5.0	30
014-05-0520 Protection of Foreign Missions and Officials			
Nondefense Discretionary Appropriation	27	5.0	1
014-05-0522 Emergencies in the Diplomatic and Consular Service			
Nondefense Discretionary Appropriation	9	5.0	*
014-05-0523 Payment to the American Institute in Taiwan			
Nondefense Discretionary Appropriation	21	5.0	1
014-05-0529 Office of the Inspector General			
Nondefense Discretionary Appropriation	129	5.0	6
014-05-0535 Embassy Security, Construction, and Maintenance			
Nondefense Discretionary Appropriation	1,579	5.0	79
014-05-0545 Representation Allowances			
Nondefense Discretionary Appropriation	7	5.0	*
014-05-0601 Repatriation Loans Program Account			
Nondefense Discretionary Appropriation	1	5.0	*
International Organizations and Conferences			
014-10-1124 Contributions for International Peacekeeping Activities			
Nondefense Discretionary Appropriation	1,839	5.0	92
014-10-1126 Contributions to International Organizations			
Nondefense Discretionary Appropriation	1,560	5.0	78
International Commissions			
014-15-1069 Salaries and Expenses, IBWC			
Nondefense Discretionary Appropriation	45	5.0	2
014-15-1078 Construction, IBWC			
Nondefense Discretionary Appropriation	32	5.0	2
014-15-1082 American Sections, International Commissions			
Nondefense Discretionary Appropriation	12	5.0	1
014-15-1087 International Fisheries Commissions			
Nondefense Discretionary Appropriation	37	5.0	2
Other			
014-25-0040 United States Emergency Refugee and Migration Assistance Fund			
Nondefense Discretionary Appropriation	27	5.0	1

Sequestrable Budgetary Resources and Reductions in Sequestrable Resources by OMB Account -- FY 2013

(Amounts in millions)

Agency / Bureau / Account / Function / BEA Category / Budgetary Resource	Sequestrable BA Amount	Sequester Percentage	Sequester Amount
014-25-0202 East-West Center			
Nondefense Discretionary Appropriation	17	5.0	1
014-25-0210 National Endowment for Democracy			
Nondefense Discretionary Appropriation	118	5.0	6
014-25-0525 Payment to the Asia Foundation			
Nondefense Discretionary Appropriation	17	5.0	1
014-25-1015 Complex Crises Fund			
Nondefense Discretionary Appropriation	40	5.0	2
014-25-1022 International Narcotics Control and Law Enforcement			
Nondefense Discretionary Appropriation	2,051	5.0	103
014-25-1031 Global Health Programs			
Nondefense Discretionary Appropriation	8,218	5.0	411
014-25-1121 Democracy Fund			
Nondefense Discretionary Appropriation	115	5.0	6
014-25-1143 Migration and Refugee Assistance			
Nondefense Discretionary Appropriation	1,885	5.0	94
014-25-8276 Israeli Arab and Eisenhower Exchange Fellowship Programs			
Nondefense Discretionary Appropriation	1	5.0	*

* denotes $500,000 or less.

Sequestrable Budgetary Resources and Reductions in Sequestrable Resources by OMB Account -- FY 2013

(Amounts in millions)

Agency / Bureau / Account / Function / BEA Category / Budgetary Resource	Sequestrable BA Amount	Sequester Percentage	Sequester Amount
Department of Transportation			
Office of the Secretary			
021-04-0102 Salaries and Expenses			
Nondefense Discretionary Appropriation	103	5.0	5
Nondefense Discretionary Spending authority	1	5.0	*
Account Total	104		5
021-04-0116 Financial Management Capital			
Nondefense Discretionary Appropriation	5	5.0	*
021-04-0118 Office of Civil Rights			
Nondefense Discretionary Appropriation	9	5.0	*
021-04-0119 Minority Business Outreach			
Nondefense Discretionary Appropriation	3	5.0	*
021-04-0142 Transportation Planning, Research, and Development			
Nondefense Discretionary Appropriation	9	5.0	*
021-04-0143 National Infrastructure Investments			
Nondefense Discretionary Appropriation	503	5.0	25
021-04-0155 Minority Business Resource Center Program			
Nondefense Discretionary Appropriation	1	5.0	*
021-04-0159 Cyber Security Initiatives			
Nondefense Discretionary Appropriation	10	5.0	1
021-04-1730 Research and Development			
Nondefense Discretionary Appropriation	16	5.0	1
021-04-5423 Essential Air Service and Rural Airport Improvement Fund			
Nondefense Mandatory Appropriation	50	5.1	3
021-04-8304 Payments to Air Carriers			
Nondefense Discretionary Appropriation	144	5.0	7
Federal Aviation Administration			
021-12-1301 Operations			
Nondefense Discretionary Appropriation	4,621	5.0	231
Nondefense Discretionary Spending authority	10	5.0	1
Account Total	4,631		232
021-12-4120 Aviation Insurance Revolving Fund			
Nondefense Mandatory Administrative expenses in otherwise exempt resources	1	5.1	*
021-12-8104 Trust Fund Share of FAA Activities (Airport and Airway Trust Fund)			
Nondefense Discretionary Appropriation	5,092	5.0	255
021-12-8106 Grants-in-aid for Airports (Airport and Airway Trust Fund)			
Nondefense Discretionary Spending authority	1	5.0	*
021-12-8107 Facilities and Equipment (Airport and Airway Trust Fund)			
Nondefense Discretionary Appropriation	2,778	5.0	139
Nondefense Discretionary Spending authority	62	5.0	3
Account Total	2,840		142
021-12-8108 Research, Engineering and Development (Airport and Airway Trust Fund)			
Nondefense Discretionary Appropriation	169	5.0	8
Federal Highway Administration			
021-15-0500 Emergency Relief Program			
Nondefense Discretionary Appropriation	2,022	5.0	101

* denotes $500,000 or less.

Sequestrable Budgetary Resources and Reductions in Sequestrable Resources by OMB Account -- FY 2013

(Amounts in millions)

Agency / Bureau / Account / Function / BEA Category / Budgetary Resource	Sequestrable BA Amount	Sequester Percentage	Sequester Amount
021-15-0534 Payment to the Transportation Trust Fund			
Nondefense Mandatory Appropriation	6,200	5.1	316
021-15-8083 Federal-aid Highways			
Nondefense Mandatory Contract authority	739	5.1	38
Federal Motor Carrier Safety Administration			
021-17-8159 Motor Carrier Safety Operations and Programs			
Nondefense Discretionary Spending authority	27	5.0	1
National Highway Traffic Safety Administration			
021-18-0650 Operations and Research			
Nondefense Discretionary Appropriation	141	5.0	7
Federal Railroad Administration			
021-27-0121 Operating Subsidy Grants to the National Railroad Passenger Corporation			
Nondefense Discretionary Appropriation	469	5.0	23
021-27-0125 Capital and Debt Service Grants to the National Railroad Passenger Corporation			
Nondefense Discretionary Appropriation	958	5.0	48
021-27-0700 Safety and Operations			
Nondefense Discretionary Appropriation	180	5.0	9
021-27-0704 Grants to the National Railroad Passenger Corporation			
Nondefense Discretionary Appropriation	118	5.0	6
021-27-0745 Railroad Research and Development			
Nondefense Discretionary Appropriation	35	5.0	2
Federal Transit Administration			
021-36-1120 Administrative Expenses			
Nondefense Discretionary Appropriation	99	5.0	5
021-36-1128 Washington Metropolitan Area Transit Authority			
Nondefense Discretionary Appropriation	151	5.0	8
021-36-1134 Capital Investment Grants			
Nondefense Discretionary Appropriation	1,923	5.0	96
021-36-1137 Research and University Research Centers			
Nondefense Discretionary Appropriation	44	5.0	2
021-36-1140 Public Transportation Emergency Relief Program			
Nondefense Discretionary Appropriation	10,894	5.0	545
Saint Lawrence Seaway Development Corporation			
021-40-8003 Operations and Maintenance			
Nondefense Discretionary Appropriation	32	5.0	2
Pipeline and Hazardous Materials Safety Administration			
021-50-1400 Operational Expenses			
Nondefense Discretionary Appropriation	20	5.0	1
021-50-1401 Hazardous Materials Safety			
Nondefense Discretionary Appropriation	42	5.0	2
021-50-5172 Pipeline Safety			
Nondefense Discretionary Appropriation	92	5.0	5
021-50-5282 Emergency Preparedness Grants			
Nondefense Mandatory Appropriation	28	5.1	1

* denotes $500,000 or less.

Sequestrable Budgetary Resources and Reductions in Sequestrable Resources by OMB Account -- FY 2013

(Amounts in millions)

Agency / Bureau / Account / Function / BEA Category / Budgetary Resource	Sequestrable BA Amount	Sequester Percentage	Sequester Amount
021-50-8121 Trust Fund Share of Pipeline Safety			
Nondefense Discretionary Appropriation	19	5.0	1
Office of Inspector General			
021-56-0130 Salaries and Expenses			
Nondefense Discretionary Appropriation	86	5.0	4
Surface Transportation Board			
021-61-0301 Salaries and Expenses			
Nondefense Discretionary Appropriation	28	5.0	1
Nondefense Discretionary Spending authority	1	5.0	*
Account Total	29		2
Maritime Administration			
021-70-1711 Maritime Security Program			
Defense Discretionary Appropriation	175	7.8	14
Defense Discretionary Unobligated balance in 050	4	7.8	*
Account Total	179		14
021-70-1750 Operations and Training			
Nondefense Discretionary Appropriation	157	5.0	8
021-70-1751 Ocean Freight Differential			
Nondefense Mandatory Borrowing authority	135	5.1	7
021-70-1752 Maritime Guaranteed Loan (title XI) Program Account			
Nondefense Discretionary Appropriation	4	5.0	*
021-70-1768 Ship Disposal			
Nondefense Discretionary Appropriation	6	5.0	*
021-70-1770 Assistance to Small Shipyards			
Nondefense Discretionary Appropriation	10	5.0	1

Agency / Bureau / Account / Function / BEA Category / Budgetary Resource	Sequestrable BA Amount	Sequester Percentage	Sequester Amount
Department of the Treasury			
Financial Crimes Enforcement Network			
015-04-0173 Salaries and Expenses			
Nondefense Discretionary Appropriation	111	5.0	6
Departmental Offices			
015-05-0101 Salaries and Expenses			
Nondefense Discretionary Appropriation	310	5.0	16
015-05-0106 Office of Inspector General			
Nondefense Discretionary Appropriation	30	5.0	2
015-05-0119 Treasury Inspector General for Tax Administration			
Nondefense Discretionary Appropriation	153	5.0	8
015-05-0123 Terrorism Insurance Program			
Nondefense Mandatory Administrative expenses in otherwise exempt resources	3	5.1	*
015-05-0126 GSE Mortgage-Backed Securities Purchase Program Account			
Nondefense Mandatory Appropriation	11	5.1	1
015-05-0140 Grants for Specified Energy Property in Lieu of Tax Credits, Recovery Act			
Nondefense Mandatory Appropriation	3,671	5.1	187
015-05-0141 Small Business Lending Fund Program Account			
Nondefense Mandatory Appropriation	26	5.1	1
015-05-1881 Community Development Financial Institutions Fund Program Account			
Nondefense Discretionary Appropriation	222	5.0	11
Nondefense Discretionary Spending authority	1	5.0	*
Account Total	223		11
015-05-5081 Presidential Election Campaign Fund			
Nondefense Mandatory Appropriation	34	5.1	2
015-05-5590 Financial Research Fund			
Nondefense Mandatory Appropriation	158	5.1	8
015-05-5697 Treasury Forfeiture Fund			
Nondefense Mandatory Appropriation	583	5.1	30
Fiscal Service			
015-12-0520 Salaries and Expenses, Fiscal Service			
Nondefense Discretionary Appropriation	393	5.0	20
Nondefense Discretionary Spending authority	1	5.0	*
Nondefense Mandatory Administrative expenses in otherwise exempt resources	68	5.1	3
Account Total	462		23
015-12-1710 Payment of Government Losses in Shipment			
Nondefense Mandatory Appropriation	1	5.1	*
015-12-1825 Payment to FRA for AMTRAK Debt Restructuring			
Nondefense Mandatory Appropriation	59	5.1	3
015-12-8209 Cheyenne River Sioux Tribe Terrestrial Wildlife Habitat Restoration Trust Fund			
Nondefense Mandatory Appropriation	2	5.1	*
Alcohol and Tobacco Tax and Trade Bureau			
015-13-1008 Salaries and Expenses			
Nondefense Discretionary Appropriation	100	5.0	5
Nondefense Discretionary Spending authority	4	5.0	*
Account Total	104		5

* denotes $500,000 or less.

Sequestrable Budgetary Resources and Reductions in Sequestrable Resources by OMB Account -- FY 2013

(Amounts in millions)

Agency / Bureau / Account / Function / BEA Category / Budgetary Resource	Sequestrable BA Amount	Sequester Percentage	Sequester Amount
Bureau of Engraving and Printing			
015-20-4502 Bureau of Engraving and Printing Fund			
Nondefense Discretionary Spending authority	643	5.0	32
United States Mint			
015-25-4159 United States Mint Public Enterprise Fund			
Nondefense Discretionary Spending authority	396	5.0	20
Internal Revenue Service			
015-45-0912 Taxpayer Services			
Nondefense Discretionary Appropriation	2,254	5.0	113
Nondefense Discretionary Spending authority	17	5.0	1
Account Total	2,271		114
015-45-0913 Enforcement			
Nondefense Discretionary Appropriation	5,331	5.0	267
Nondefense Discretionary Spending authority	17	5.0	1
Account Total	5,348		267
015-45-0919 Operations Support			
Nondefense Discretionary Appropriation	3,971	5.0	199
Nondefense Discretionary Spending authority	12	5.0	1
Account Total	3,983		199
015-45-0921 Business Systems Modernization			
Nondefense Discretionary Appropriation	332	5.0	17
015-45-0935 Build America Bond Payments, Recovery Act			
Nondefense Mandatory Appropriation	3,351	5.1	171
015-45-0945 Payment to Issuer of Qualified Zone Academy Bonds			
Nondefense Mandatory Appropriation	38	5.1	2
015-45-0946 Payment to Issuer of Qualified School Construction Bonds			
Nondefense Mandatory Appropriation	820	5.1	42
015-45-0947 Payment to Issuer of New Clean Renewable Energy Bonds			
Nondefense Mandatory Appropriation	24	5.1	1
015-45-0948 Payment to Issuer of Qualified Energy Conservation Bonds			
Nondefense Mandatory Appropriation	32	5.1	2
015-45-0951 Payment Where Small Business Health Insurance Tax Credit Exceeds Liability for Tax			
Nondefense Mandatory Appropriation	127	5.1	6
015-45-5432 IRS Miscellaneous Retained Fees			
Nondefense Mandatory Appropriation	39	5.1	2
015-45-5433 Informant Payments			
Nondefense Mandatory Appropriation	125	5.1	6

Agency / Bureau / Account / Function / BEA Category / Budgetary Resource	Sequestrable BA Amount	Sequester Percentage	Sequester Amount
Corps of Engineers--Civil Works			
202-00-3112 Mississippi River and Tributaries			
Nondefense　Discretionary　Appropriation	252	5.0	13
202-00-3121 Investigations			
Nondefense　Discretionary　Appropriation	176	5.0	9
202-00-3122 Construction			
Nondefense　Discretionary　Appropriation	5,007	5.0	250
202-00-3123 Operation and Maintenance			
Nondefense　Discretionary　Appropriation	2,448	5.0	122
202-00-3124 Expenses			
Nondefense　Discretionary　Appropriation	196	5.0	10
202-00-3125 Flood Control and Coastal Emergencies			
Nondefense　Discretionary　Appropriation	1,035	5.0	52
202-00-3126 Regulatory Program			
Nondefense　Discretionary　Appropriation	194	5.0	10
202-00-3130 Formerly Utilized Sites Remedial Action Program			
Defense　Discretionary　Appropriation	110	7.8	9
Defense　Discretionary　Unobligated balance in 050	4	7.8	*
Account Total	114		9
202-00-3132 Office of the Assistant Secretary of the Army for Civil Works			
Defense　Discretionary　Appropriation	5	7.8	*
202-00-4902 Revolving Fund			
Nondefense　Mandatory　Administrative expenses in otherwise exempt resources	3	5.1	*
202-00-8217 South Dakota Terrestrial Wildlife Habitat Restoration Trust Fund			
Nondefense　Mandatory　Appropriation	5	5.1	*
202-00-8333 Coastal Wetlands Restoration Trust Fund			
Nondefense　Mandatory　Appropriation	81	5.1	4
202-00-8861 Inland Waterways Trust Fund			
Nondefense　Discretionary　Appropriation	77	5.0	4
202-00-8862 Rivers and Harbors Contributed Funds			
Nondefense　Mandatory　Administrative expenses in otherwise exempt resources	267	5.1	14
202-00-8863 Harbor Maintenance Trust Fund			
Nondefense　Discretionary　Appropriation	882	5.0	44
202-00-9921 Permanent Appropriations			
Nondefense　Mandatory　Appropriation	21	5.1	1

Agency / Bureau / Account / Function / BEA Category / Budgetary Resource	Sequestrable BA Amount	Sequester Percentage	Sequester Amount
Other Defense Civil Programs			
American Battle Monuments Commission			
200-15-0100 Salaries and Expenses			
Nondefense Discretionary Appropriation	77	5.0	4
Armed Forces Retirement Home			
200-20-8522 Armed Forces Retirement Home			
Nondefense Discretionary Appropriation	62	5.0	3
Cemeterial Expenses			
200-25-1805 Salaries and Expenses			
Nondefense Discretionary Appropriation	46	5.0	2
Forest and Wildlife Conservation, Military Reservations			
200-30-5095 Wildlife Conservation			
Nondefense Mandatory Administrative expenses in otherwise exempt resources	3	5.1	*
Selective Service System			
200-45-0400 Salaries and Expenses			
Defense Discretionary Appropriation	24	7.8	2

Agency / Bureau / Account / Function / BEA Category / Budgetary Resource	Sequestrable BA Amount	Sequester Percentage	Sequester Amount
Environmental Protection Agency			
020-00-0103 State and Tribal Assistance Grants			
Nondefense Discretionary Appropriation	4,190	5.0	210
020-00-0107 Science and Technology			
Nondefense Discretionary Appropriation	799	5.0	40
020-00-0108 Environmental Programs and Management			
Nondefense Discretionary Appropriation	2,696	5.0	135
020-00-0110 Buildings and Facilities			
Nondefense Discretionary Appropriation	37	5.0	2
020-00-0112 Office of Inspector General			
Nondefense Discretionary Appropriation	42	5.0	2
020-00-4310 Reregistration and Expedited Processing Revolving Fund			
Nondefense Mandatory Spending authority	28	5.1	1
020-00-5374 Pesticide Registration Fund			
Nondefense Discretionary Appropriation	15	5.0	1
020-00-8145 Hazardous Substance Superfund			
Nondefense Discretionary Appropriation	1,218	5.0	61
Nondefense Discretionary Spending authority	240	5.0	12
Nondefense Mandatory Appropriation	25	5.1	1
Account Total	1,483		74
020-00-8153 Leaking Underground Storage Tank Trust Fund			
Nondefense Discretionary Appropriation	110	5.0	6
020-00-8221 Inland Oil Spill Programs			
Nondefense Discretionary Appropriation	18	5.0	1

Sequestrable Budgetary Resources and Reductions in Sequestrable Resources by OMB Account -- FY 2013

(Amounts in millions)

Agency / Bureau / Account / Function / BEA Category / Budgetary Resource	Sequestrable BA Amount	Sequester Percentage	Sequester Amount
Executive Office of the President			
The White House			
100-05-0209 The White House			
Nondefense Discretionary Appropriation	57	5.0	3
Executive Residence at the White House			
100-10-0109 White House Repair and Restoration			
Nondefense Discretionary Appropriation	1	5.0	*
100-10-0210 Operating Expenses			
Nondefense Discretionary Appropriation	13	5.0	1
Nondefense Discretionary Spending authority	3	5.0	*
Account Total	16		1
Special Assistance to the President and the Official Residence of the Vice President			
100-15-1454 Special Assistance to the President and the Official Residence of the Vice President			
Nondefense Discretionary Appropriation	5	5.0	*
Council of Economic Advisers			
100-20-1900 Salaries and Expenses			
Nondefense Discretionary Appropriation	4	5.0	*
Council on Environmental Quality and Office of Environmental Quality			
100-25-1453 Council on Environmental Quality and Office of Environmental Quality			
Nondefense Discretionary Appropriation	3	5.0	*
National Security Council and Homeland Security Council			
100-35-2000 Salaries and Expenses			
Nondefense Discretionary Appropriation	13	5.0	1
Office of Administration			
100-50-0038 Salaries and Expenses			
Nondefense Discretionary Appropriation	114	5.0	6
Office of Management and Budget			
100-55-0300 Office of Management and Budget			
Nondefense Discretionary Appropriation	90	5.0	5
Office of National Drug Control Policy			
100-60-1457 Office of National Drug Control Policy			
Nondefense Discretionary Appropriation	25	5.0	1
Office of Science and Technology Policy			
100-65-2600 Office of Science and Technology Policy			
Nondefense Discretionary Appropriation	5	5.0	*
Office of the United States Trade Representative			
100-70-0400 Office of the United States Trade Representative			
Nondefense Discretionary Appropriation	52	5.0	3
Unanticipated Needs			
100-95-0037 Unanticipated Needs			
Nondefense Discretionary Appropriation	1	5.0	*

* denotes $500,000 or less.

Agency / Bureau / Account / Function / BEA Category / Budgetary Resource	Sequestrable BA Amount	Sequester Percentage	Sequester Amount
General Services Administration			
Real Property Activities			
023-05-4542 Federal Buildings Fund			
Nondefense Discretionary Appropriation	7	5.0	*
023-05-5254 Disposal of Surplus Real and Related Personal Property			
Nondefense Mandatory Appropriation	9	5.1	*
Supply and Technology Activities			
023-10-5250 Expenses of Transportation Audit Contracts and Contract Administration			
Nondefense Mandatory Appropriation	13	5.1	1
General Activities			
023-30-0105 Allowances and Office Staff for Former Presidents			
Nondefense Discretionary Appropriation	3	5.0	*
023-30-0108 Office of Inspector General			
Nondefense Discretionary Appropriation	58	5.0	3
023-30-0110 Operating Expenses			
Nondefense Discretionary Appropriation	70	5.0	4
023-30-0401 Government-wide Policy			
Nondefense Discretionary Appropriation	61	5.0	3
023-30-0600 Electronic Government (E-GOV) Fund			
Nondefense Discretionary Appropriation	12	5.0	1
023-30-4549 Federal Citizen Services Fund			
Nondefense Discretionary Appropriation	34	5.0	2

* denotes $500,000 or less.

Agency / Bureau / Account / Function / BEA Category / Budgetary Resource	Sequestrable BA Amount	Sequester Percentage	Sequester Amount
International Assistance Programs			
Millennium Challenge Corporation			
184-03-2750 Millennium Challenge Corporation			
Nondefense Discretionary Appropriation	904	5.0	45
International Security Assistance			
184-05-1032 Peacekeeping Operations			
Nondefense Discretionary Appropriation	386	5.0	19
184-05-1037 Economic Support Fund			
Nondefense Discretionary Appropriation	5,675	5.0	284
184-05-1075 Nonproliferation, Antiterrorism, Demining, and Related Programs			
Nondefense Discretionary Appropriation	714	5.0	36
184-05-1081 International Military Education and Training			
Nondefense Discretionary Appropriation	106	5.0	5
184-05-1082 Foreign Military Financing Program			
Nondefense Discretionary Appropriation	6,344	5.0	317
184-05-1083 Pakistan Counterinsurgency Capability Fund			
Nondefense Discretionary Appropriation	850	5.0	43
Multilateral Assistance			
184-10-0071 Strategic Climate Fund			
Nondefense Discretionary Appropriation	50	5.0	3
184-10-0072 Contribution to the Inter-American Development Bank			
Nondefense Discretionary Appropriation	80	5.0	4
184-10-0073 Contribution to the International Development Association			
Nondefense Discretionary Appropriation	1,501	5.0	75
184-10-0076 Contribution to the Asian Development Bank			
Nondefense Discretionary Appropriation	208	5.0	10
184-10-0077 Contribution to the International Bank for Reconstruction and Development			
Nondefense Discretionary Appropriation	208	5.0	10
184-10-0080 Clean Technology Fund			
Nondefense Discretionary Appropriation	186	5.0	9
184-10-0082 Contribution to the African Development Bank			
Nondefense Discretionary Appropriation	214	5.0	11
184-10-0089 Contribution to Enterprise for the Americas Multilateral Investment Fund			
Nondefense Discretionary Appropriation	25	5.0	1
184-10-0091 Debt Restructuring			
Nondefense Discretionary Appropriation	12	5.0	1
184-10-1005 International Organizations and Programs			
Nondefense Discretionary Appropriation	351	5.0	18
184-10-1039 Contributions to the International Fund for Agricultural Development			
Nondefense Discretionary Appropriation	30	5.0	2
184-10-1045 International Affairs Technical Assistance Program			
Nondefense Discretionary Appropriation	27	5.0	1
184-10-1475 Global Food Security Fund			
Nondefense Discretionary Appropriation	136	5.0	7

* denotes $500,000 or less.

(Amounts in millions)

Agency / Bureau / Account / Function / BEA Category / Budgetary Resource	Sequestrable BA Amount	Sequester Percentage	Sequester Amount
Agency for International Development			
184-15-0300 Capital Investment Fund of the United States Agency for International Development.			
Nondefense Discretionary Appropriation	130	5.0	7
184-15-0306 Assistance for Europe, Eurasia and Central Asia			
Nondefense Discretionary Appropriation	631	5.0	32
184-15-1000 Operating Expenses of the Agency for International Development			
Nondefense Discretionary Appropriation	1,354	5.0	68
184-15-1007 Operating Expenses, Office of Inspector General			
Nondefense Discretionary Appropriation	51	5.0	3
184-15-1021 Development Assistance Program			
Nondefense Discretionary Appropriation	2,535	5.0	127
184-15-1027 Transition Initiatives			
Nondefense Discretionary Appropriation	57	5.0	3
184-15-1035 International Disaster Assistance			
Nondefense Discretionary Appropriation	980	5.0	49
184-15-1264 Development Credit Authority Program Account			
Nondefense Discretionary Appropriation	8	5.0	*
Overseas Private Investment Corporation			
184-20-0100 Overseas Private Investment Corporation Program Account			
Nondefense Discretionary Spending authority	58	5.0	3
Trade and Development Agency			
184-25-1001 Trade and Development Agency			
Nondefense Discretionary Appropriation	50	5.0	3
Peace Corps			
184-35-0100 Peace Corps			
Nondefense Discretionary Appropriation	377	5.0	19
Inter-American Foundation			
184-40-3100 Inter-American Foundation			
Nondefense Discretionary Appropriation	23	5.0	1
Nondefense Discretionary Spending authority	6	5.0	*
Account Total	29		2
African Development Foundation			
184-50-0700 African Development Foundation			
Nondefense Discretionary Appropriation	30	5.0	2
Military Sales Program			
184-70-8242 Foreign Military Sales Trust Fund			
Nondefense Mandatory Administrative expenses in otherwise exempt resources	147	5.1	7

* denotes $500,000 or less.

Sequestrable Budgetary Resources and Reductions in Sequestrable Resources by OMB Account -- FY 2013

(Amounts in millions)

Agency / Bureau / Account / Function / BEA Category / Budgetary Resource	Sequestrable BA Amount	Sequester Percentage	Sequester Amount
National Aeronautics and Space Administration			
026-00-0109 Office of Inspector General			
Nondefense Discretionary Appropriation	39	5.0	2
026-00-0115 Space Operations			
Nondefense Discretionary Appropriation	4,247	5.0	212
026-00-0120 Science			
Nondefense Discretionary Appropriation	5,116	5.0	256
026-00-0122 Cross Agency Support			
Nondefense Discretionary Appropriation	3,012	5.0	151
026-00-0124 Exploration			
Nondefense Discretionary Appropriation	3,790	5.0	190
026-00-0126 Aeronautics			
Nondefense Discretionary Appropriation	573	5.0	29
026-00-0128 Education			
Nondefense Discretionary Appropriation	137	5.0	7
026-00-0130 Construction, Environmental Compliance, and Remediation			
Nondefense Discretionary Appropriation	402	5.0	20
026-00-0131 Space Technology			
Nondefense Discretionary Appropriation	579	5.0	29
026-00-8978 Science, Space, and Technology Education Trust Fund			
Nondefense Mandatory Appropriation	1	5.1	*

Agency / Bureau / Account / Function / BEA Category / Budgetary Resource	Sequestrable BA Amount	Sequester Percentage	Sequester Amount
National Science Foundation			
422-00-0100 Research and Related Activities			
Defense Discretionary Appropriation	68	7.8	5
Nondefense Discretionary Appropriation	5,686	5.0	284
Account Total	5,754		290
422-00-0106 Education and Human Resources			
Nondefense Discretionary Appropriation	834	5.0	42
Nondefense Mandatory Appropriation	100	5.1	5
Account Total	934		47
422-00-0180 Agency Operations and Award Management			
Nondefense Discretionary Appropriation	301	5.0	15
422-00-0300 Office of the Inspector General			
Nondefense Discretionary Appropriation	14	5.0	1
422-00-0350 Office of the National Science Board			
Nondefense Discretionary Appropriation	4	5.0	*
422-00-0551 Major Research Equipment and Facilities Construction			
Nondefense Discretionary Appropriation	168	5.0	8
422-00-8960 Donations			
Nondefense Mandatory Administrative expenses in otherwise exempt resources	9	5.1	*

* denotes $500,000 or less.

Sequestrable Budgetary Resources and Reductions in Sequestrable Resources by OMB Account -- FY 2013

(Amounts in millions)

Agency / Bureau / Account / Function / BEA Category / Budgetary Resource	Sequestrable BA Amount	Sequester Percentage	Sequester Amount
Office of Personnel Management			
027-00-0100 Salaries and Expenses			
Nondefense Discretionary Appropriation	99	5.0	5
027-00-0400 Office of Inspector General			
Nondefense Discretionary Appropriation	3	5.0	*
027-00-0800 Flexible Benefits Plan Reserve			
Nondefense Mandatory Spending authority	30	5.1	2
027-00-8135 Civil Service Retirement and Disability Fund			
Nondefense Mandatory Administrative expenses in otherwise exempt resources	48	5.1	2
027-00-8424 Employees Life Insurance Fund			
Nondefense Mandatory Administrative expenses in otherwise exempt resources	2	5.1	*
027-00-9981 Employees and Retired Employees Health Benefits Funds			
Nondefense Mandatory Administrative expenses in otherwise exempt resources	17	5.1	1

Sequestrable Budgetary Resources and Reductions in Sequestrable Resources by OMB Account -- FY 2013

(Amounts in millions)

Agency / Bureau / Account / Function / BEA Category / Budgetary Resource	Sequestrable BA Amount	Sequester Percentage	Sequester Amount
Small Business Administration			
028-00-0100 Salaries and Expenses			
Nondefense Discretionary Appropriation	440	5.0	22
028-00-0200 Office of Inspector General			
Nondefense Discretionary Appropriation	21	5.0	1
028-00-0300 Office of Advocacy			
Nondefense Discretionary Appropriation	9	5.0	*
028-00-1152 Disaster Loans Program Account			
Nondefense Discretionary Appropriation	896	5.0	45
028-00-1154 Business Loans Program Account			
Nondefense Discretionary Appropriation	487	5.0	24

* denotes $500,000 or less.

Sequestrable Budgetary Resources and Reductions in Sequestrable Resources by OMB Account -- FY 2013

(Amounts in millions)

Agency / Bureau / Account / Function / BEA Category / Budgetary Resource	Sequestrable BA Amount	Sequester Percentage	Sequester Amount
Social Security Administration			
016-00-0400 Office of the Inspector General			
Nondefense Discretionary Appropriation	29	5.0	1
016-00-8006 Federal Old-age and Survivors Insurance Trust Fund			
Nondefense Discretionary Appropriation	2,744	5.0	137
016-00-8007 Federal Disability Insurance Trust Fund			
Nondefense Discretionary Appropriation	2,954	5.0	148

* denotes $500,000 or less.

Sequestrable Budgetary Resources and Reductions in Sequestrable Resources by OMB Account -- FY 2013

(Amounts in millions)

Agency / Bureau / Account / Function / BEA Category / Budgetary Resource	Sequestrable BA Amount	Sequester Percentage	Sequester Amount
Access Board			
Architectural and Transportation Barriers Compliance Board			
310-00-3200 Salaries and Expenses			
Nondefense Discretionary Appropriation	7	5.0	*
Administrative Conference of the United States			
302-00-1700 Salaries and Expenses			
Nondefense Discretionary Appropriation	3	5.0	*
Advisory Council on Historic Preservation			
306-00-2300 Salaries and Expenses			
Nondefense Discretionary Appropriation	6	5.0	*
Affordable Housing Program			
530-00-5528 Affordable Housing Program			
Nondefense Mandatory Appropriation	198	5.1	10
Appalachian Regional Commission			
309-00-0200 Appalachian Regional Commission			
Nondefense Discretionary Appropriation	64	5.0	3
309-00-9971 Miscellaneous Trust Funds			
Nondefense Mandatory Appropriation	8	5.1	*
Broadcasting Board of Governors			
514-00-0204 Broadcasting Capital Improvements			
Nondefense Discretionary Appropriation	7	5.0	*
514-00-0206 International Broadcasting Operations			
Nondefense Discretionary Appropriation	749	5.0	37
Bureau of Consumer Financial Protection			
581-00-5577 Bureau of Consumer Financial Protection Fund			
Nondefense Mandatory Appropriation	448	5.1	23
Chemical Safety and Hazard Investigation Board			
510-00-3850 Chemical Safety and Hazard Investigation Board			
Nondefense Discretionary Appropriation	11	5.0	1
Christopher Columbus Fellowship Foundation			
465-00-0100 Payment to the Christopher Columbus Fellowship Foundation			
Nondefense Discretionary Appropriation	*	5.0	*
Commission of Fine Arts			
323-00-2600 Salaries and Expenses			
Nondefense Discretionary Appropriation	2	5.0	*
323-00-2602 National Capital Arts and Cultural Affairs			
Nondefense Discretionary Appropriation	2	5.0	*
Commission on Civil Rights			
326-00-1900 Salaries and Expenses			
Nondefense Discretionary Appropriation	9	5.0	*
Committee for Purchase from People Who Are Blind or Severely Disabled			
Committee for Purchase from People who are Blind or Severely Disabled, activities			

* denotes $500,000 or less.

Sequestrable Budgetary Resources and Reductions in Sequestrable Resources by OMB Account -- FY 2013

(Amounts in millions)

Agency / Bureau / Account / Function / BEA Category / Budgetary Resource			Sequestrable BA Amount	Sequester Percentage	Sequester Amount
338-00-2000 Salaries and Expenses					
Nondefense	Discretionary	Appropriation	5	5.0	*
Commodity Futures Trading Commission					
339-00-1400 Commodity Futures Trading Commission					
Nondefense	Discretionary	Appropriation	206	5.0	10
339-00-4334 Customer Protection Fund					
Nondefense	Mandatory	Spending authority	13	5.1	1
Consumer Product Safety Commission					
343-00-0100 Salaries and Expenses					
Nondefense	Discretionary	Appropriation	115	5.0	6
Corporation for National and Community Service					
485-00-2721 Inspector General					
Nondefense	Discretionary	Appropriation	4	5.0	*
485-00-2722 Salaries and Expenses					
Nondefense	Discretionary	Appropriation	83	5.0	4
485-00-2726 Payment to National Service Trust Fund					
Nondefense	Discretionary	Appropriation	213	5.0	11
485-00-2728 Operating Expenses					
Nondefense	Discretionary	Appropriation	755	5.0	38
Corporation for Public Broadcasting					
344-00-0151 Corporation for Public Broadcasting					
Nondefense	Discretionary	Advance appropriation	445	5.0	22
Corporation for Travel Promotion					
580-00-5585 Travel Promotion Fund					
Nondefense	Mandatory	Appropriation	100	5.1	5
Court Services and Offender Supervision Agency for the District of Columbia					
511-00-1733 Public Defender Service for the District of Columbia					
Nondefense	Discretionary	Appropriation	37	5.0	2
511-00-1734 Federal Payment to Court Services and Offender Supervision Agency for the District of Columbia					
Nondefense	Discretionary	Appropriation	214	5.0	11
Defense Nuclear Facilities Safety Board					
347-00-3900 Salaries and Expenses					
Defense	Discretionary	Appropriation	29	7.8	2
Defense	Discretionary	Unobligated balance in 050	1	7.8	*
		Account Total	30		2
Delta Regional Authority					
517-00-0750 Delta Regional Authority					
Nondefense	Discretionary	Appropriation	12	5.0	1
Denali Commission					
513-00-1200 Denali Commission					
Nondefense	Discretionary	Appropriation	12	5.0	1
513-00-8056 Denali Commission Trust Fund					
Nondefense	Discretionary	Appropriation	4	5.0	*
District of Columbia					

* denotes $500,000 or less.

Agency / Bureau / Account / Function / BEA Category / Budgetary Resource			Sequestrable BA Amount	Sequester Percentage	Sequester Amount
District of Columbia Courts					
349-10-1712 Federal Payment to the District of Columbia Courts					
Nondefense	Discretionary	Appropriation	234	5.0	12
Nondefense	Discretionary	Spending authority	1	5.0	*
		Account Total	235		12
349-10-1736 Defender Services in District of Columbia Courts					
Nondefense	Discretionary	Appropriation	55	5.0	3
349-10-8212 District of Columbia Judicial Retirement and Survivors Annuity Fund					
Nondefense	Mandatory	Administrative expenses in otherwise exempt resources	1	5.1	*
District of Columbia General and Special Payments					
349-30-1707 Federal Support for Economic Development and Management Reforms in the District					
Nondefense	Discretionary	Appropriation	23	5.0	1
349-30-1736 Federal Payment for Resident Tuition Support					
Nondefense	Discretionary	Appropriation	30	5.0	2
349-30-1771 Federal Payment for Emergency Planning and Security Cost in the District of Columbia					
Nondefense	Discretionary	Appropriation	25	5.0	1
349-30-1817 Federal Payment for School Improvement					
Nondefense	Discretionary	Appropriation	60	5.0	3
349-30-5511 District of Columbia Federal Pension Fund					
Nondefense	Mandatory	Administrative expenses in otherwise exempt resources	17	5.1	1
Election Assistance Commission					
525-00-1650 Salaries and Expenses					
Nondefense	Discretionary	Appropriation	9	5.0	*
Electric Reliability Organization					
531-00-5522 Electric Reliability Organization					
Nondefense	Mandatory	Appropriation	100	5.1	5
Equal Employment Opportunity Commission					
350-00-0100 Salaries and Expenses					
Nondefense	Discretionary	Appropriation	362	5.0	18
350-00-4019 EEOC Education, Technical Assistance, and Training Revolving Fund					
Nondefense	Mandatory	Administrative expenses in otherwise exempt resources	4	5.1	*
Export-Import Bank of the United States					
351-00-0105 Inspector General of the Export-Import Bank					
Nondefense	Discretionary	Appropriation	4	5.0	*
Farm Credit System Insurance Corporation					
355-00-4171 Farm Credit System Insurance Fund					
Nondefense	Mandatory	Administrative expenses in otherwise exempt resources	4	5.1	*
Federal Communications Commission					
356-00-0100 Salaries and Expenses					
Nondefense	Discretionary	Spending authority	342	5.0	17
356-00-0300 Spectrum Auction Program Account					
Nondefense	Mandatory	Appropriation	4	5.1	*
Federal Deposit Insurance Corporation					
Orderly Liquidation					

* denotes $500,000 or less.

Sequestrable Budgetary Resources and Reductions in Sequestrable Resources by OMB Account -- FY 2013

(Amounts in millions)

Agency / Bureau / Account / Function / BEA Category / Budgetary Resource	Sequestrable BA Amount	Sequester Percentage	Sequester Amount
357-35-5586 Orderly Liquidation Fund			
Nondefense Mandatory Appropriation	161	5.1	8
Nondefense Mandatory Borrowing authority	1,354	5.1	69
Account Total	1,515		77
Federal Drug Control Programs			
154-00-1070 High-intensity Drug Trafficking Areas Program			
Nondefense Discretionary Appropriation	240	5.0	12
154-00-1460 Other Federal Drug Control Programs			
Nondefense Discretionary Appropriation	101	5.0	5
Federal Election Commission			
360-00-1600 Salaries and Expenses			
Nondefense Discretionary Appropriation	67	5.0	3
Federal Financial Institutions Examination Council			
Federal Financial Institutions Examination Council Appraisal Subcommittee			
362-20-5026 Registry Fees			
Nondefense Mandatory Appropriation	2	5.1	*
Federal Labor Relations Authority			
365-00-0100 Salaries and Expenses			
Nondefense Discretionary Appropriation	25	5.0	1
Federal Maritime Commission			
366-00-0100 Salaries and Expenses			
Nondefense Discretionary Appropriation	24	5.0	1
Federal Mediation and Conciliation Service			
367-00-0100 Salaries and Expenses			
Nondefense Discretionary Appropriation	46	5.0	2
Nondefense Discretionary Spending authority	1	5.0	*
Account Total	47		2
Federal Mine Safety and Health Review Commission			
368-00-2800 Salaries and Expenses			
Nondefense Discretionary Appropriation	18	5.0	1
Federal Trade Commission			
370-00-0100 Salaries and Expenses			
Nondefense Discretionary Appropriation	185	5.0	9
Nondefense Discretionary Spending authority	129	5.0	6
Account Total	314		16
Harry S Truman Scholarship Foundation			
372-00-0950 Payment to the Harry S. Truman Scholarship Memorial Trust Fund			
Nondefense Discretionary Appropriation	1	5.0	*
Institute of American Indian and Alaska Native Culture and Arts Development			
373-00-2900 Payment to the Institute			
Nondefense Discretionary Appropriation	9	5.0	*
Institute of Museum and Library Services			
474-00-0300 Office of Museum and Library Services: Grants and Administration			
Nondefense Discretionary Appropriation	233	5.0	12
Intelligence Community Management Account			

* denotes $500,000 or less.

Agency / Bureau / Account / Function / BEA Category / Budgetary Resource	Sequestrable BA Amount	Sequester Percentage	Sequester Amount
467-00-0401 Intelligence Community Management Account			
Defense Discretionary Appropriation	551	7.8	43
International Trade Commission			
378-00-0100 Salaries and Expenses			
Nondefense Discretionary Appropriation	80	5.0	4
Legal Services Corporation			
385-00-0501 Payment to Legal Services Corporation			
Nondefense Discretionary Appropriation	351	5.0	18
Marine Mammal Commission			
387-00-2200 Salaries and Expenses			
Nondefense Discretionary Appropriation	3	5.0	*
Merit Systems Protection Board			
389-00-0100 Salaries and Expenses			
Nondefense Discretionary Appropriation	40	5.0	2
Morris K. Udall and Stewart L. Udall Foundation			
487-00-0900 Federal Payment to Morris K. Udall and Stewart L. Udall Foundation Trust Fund			
Nondefense Discretionary Appropriation	2	5.0	*
487-00-5415 Environmental Dispute Resolution Fund			
Nondefense Discretionary Appropriation	4	5.0	*
Nondefense Mandatory Administrative expenses in otherwise exempt resources	3	5.1	*
Account Total	7		*
National Archives and Records Administration			
393-00-0300 Operating Expenses			
Nondefense Discretionary Appropriation	375	5.0	19
393-00-0301 National Historical Publications and Records Commission			
Nondefense Discretionary Appropriation	5	5.0	*
393-00-0302 Repairs and Restoration			
Nondefense Discretionary Appropriation	9	5.0	*
393-00-0305 Office of the Inspector General - National Archives and Records Adminsitration			
Nondefense Discretionary Appropriation	4	5.0	*
393-00-8436 National Archives Trust Fund			
Nondefense Mandatory Administrative expenses in otherwise exempt resources	1	5.1	*
National Capital Planning Commission			
394-00-2500 Salaries and Expenses			
Nondefense Discretionary Appropriation	8	5.0	*
National Council on Disability			
413-00-3500 Salaries and Expenses			
Nondefense Discretionary Appropriation	3	5.0	*
National Credit Union Administration			
415-00-4472 Community Development Credit Union Revolving Loan Fund			
Nondefense Discretionary Appropriation	1	5.0	*
National Endowment for the Arts			
417-00-0100 National Endowment for the Arts: Grants and Administration			
Nondefense Discretionary Appropriation	147	5.0	7

* denotes $500,000 or less.

Sequestrable Budgetary Resources and Reductions in Sequestrable Resources by OMB Account -- FY 2013

(Amounts in millions)

Agency / Bureau / Account / Function / BEA Category / Budgetary Resource	Sequestrable BA Amount	Sequester Percentage	Sequester Amount
National Endowment for the Humanities			
418-00-0200 National Endowment for the Humanities: Grants and Administration			
Nondefense Discretionary Appropriation	147	5.0	7
National Labor Relations Board			
420-00-0100 Salaries and Expenses			
Nondefense Discretionary Appropriation	280	5.0	14
National Mediation Board			
421-00-2400 Salaries and Expenses			
Nondefense Discretionary Appropriation	13	5.0	1
National Railroad Passenger Corporation Office of Inspector General			
575-00-2996 Salaries and Expenses			
Nondefense Discretionary Appropriation	21	5.0	1
National Transportation Safety Board			
424-00-0310 Salaries and Expenses			
Nondefense Discretionary Appropriation	103	5.0	5
Neighborhood Reinvestment Corporation			
428-00-1300 Payment to Neighborhood Reinvestment Corporation			
Nondefense Discretionary Appropriation	216	5.0	11
Northern Border Regional Commission			
573-00-3742 Northern Border Regional Commission			
Nondefense Discretionary Appropriation	1	5.0	*
Nuclear Regulatory Commission			
429-00-0200 Salaries and Expenses			
Nondefense Discretionary Appropriation	1,033	5.0	52
Nondefense Discretionary Spending authority	6	5.0	*
Account Total	1,039		52
429-00-0300 Office of Inspector General			
Nondefense Discretionary Appropriation	11	5.0	1
Nuclear Waste Technical Review Board			
431-00-0500 Salaries and Expenses			
Nondefense Discretionary Appropriation	3	5.0	*
Occupational Safety and Health Review Commission			
432-00-2100 Salaries and Expenses			
Nondefense Discretionary Appropriation	12	5.0	1
Office of Government Ethics			
434-00-1100 Salaries and Expenses			
Nondefense Discretionary Appropriation	19	5.0	1
Nondefense Discretionary Spending authority	1	5.0	*
Account Total	20		1
Office of Navajo and Hopi Indian Relocation			
435-00-1100 Salaries and Expenses			
Nondefense Discretionary Appropriation	8	5.0	*
Office of Special Counsel			

* denotes $500,000 or less.

(Amounts in millions)

Agency / Bureau / Account / Function / BEA Category / Budgetary Resource			Sequestrable BA Amount	Sequester Percentage	Sequester Amount
436-00-0100 Salaries and Expenses					
Nondefense	Discretionary	Appropriation	19	5.0	1
Office of the Federal Coordinator for Alaska Natural Gas Transportation Projects					
534-00-2850 Office of the Federal Coordinator for Alaska Natural Gas Transportation					
Nondefense	Discretionary	Appropriation	1	5.0	*
Nondefense	Mandatory	Administrative expenses in otherwise exempt resources	2	5.1	*
		Account Total	3		*
Other Commissions and Boards					
505-00-9911 Other Commissions and Boards					
Nondefense	Discretionary	Appropriation	1	5.0	*
Patient-Centered Outcomes Research Trust Fund					
579-00-8299 Patient-Centered Outcomes Research Trust Fund					
Nondefense	Mandatory	Appropriation	390	5.1	20
Postal Service					
440-00-1001 Payment to Postal Service Fund					
Nondefense	Discretionary	Advance appropriation	78	5.0	4
Presidio Trust					
512-00-4331 Presidio Trust					
Nondefense	Discretionary	Appropriation	12	5.0	1
Privacy and Civil Liberties Oversight Board					
535-00-2724 Salaries and Expenses					
Defense	Discretionary	Appropriation	1	7.8	*
Railroad Retirement Board					
446-00-8010 Railroad Social Security Equivalent Benefit Account					
Nondefense	Discretionary	Appropriation	34	5.0	2
446-00-8051 Railroad Unemployment Insurance Trust Fund					
Nondefense	Discretionary	Appropriation	15	5.0	1
Nondefense	Mandatory	Appropriation	99	5.1	5
Nondefense	Mandatory	Spending authority	20	5.1	1
		Account Total	134		7
Recovery Accountability and Transparency Board					
Recovery Act Accountability and Transparency Board					
539-00-3725 Recovery Act Accountability and Transparency Board, Recovery Act					
Nondefense	Discretionary	Appropriation	28	5.0	1
Securities and Exchange Commission					
449-00-0100 Salaries and Expenses					
Nondefense	Discretionary	Spending authority	1,321	5.0	66
449-00-5566 Securities and Exchange Commission Reserve Fund					
Nondefense	Mandatory	Appropriation	50	5.1	3
449-00-5567 Investor Protection Fund					
Nondefense	Mandatory	Appropriation	90	5.1	5
Public Company Accounting Oversight Board					

Sequestrable Budgetary Resources and Reductions in Sequestrable Resources by OMB Account -- FY 2013

(Amounts in millions)

Agency / Bureau / Account / Function / BEA Category / Budgetary Resource	Sequestrable BA Amount	Sequester Percentage	Sequester Amount
526-00-5376 Public Company Accounting Oversight Board			
Nondefense Discretionary Appropriation	1	5.0	*
Nondefense Mandatory Appropriation	236	5.1	12
Account Total	237		12
Standard Setting Body			
527-00-5377 Payment to Standard Setting Body			
Nondefense Mandatory Appropriation	25	5.1	1
Securities Investor Protection Corporation			
576-00-5600 Securities Investor Protection Corporation			
Nondefense Mandatory Appropriation	299	5.1	15
Smithsonian Institution			
452-00-0100 Salaries and Expenses			
Nondefense Discretionary Appropriation	642	5.0	32
452-00-0103 Facilities Capital			
Nondefense Discretionary Appropriation	176	5.0	9
452-00-0200 Salaries and Expenses, National Gallery of Art			
Nondefense Discretionary Appropriation	115	5.0	6
452-00-0201 Repair, Restoration, and Renovation of Buildings, National Gallery of Art			
Nondefense Discretionary Appropriation	15	5.0	1
452-00-0302 Operations and Maintenance, JFK Center for the Performing Arts			
Nondefense Discretionary Appropriation	23	5.0	1
452-00-0303 Capital Repair and Restoration, JFK Center for the Performing Arts			
Nondefense Discretionary Appropriation	14	5.0	1
452-00-0400 Salaries and Expenses, Woodrow Wilson International Center for Scholars			
Nondefense Discretionary Appropriation	11	5.0	1
State Justice Institute			
453-00-0052 State Justice Institute: Salaries and Expenses			
Nondefense Discretionary Appropriation	5	5.0	*
Tennessee Valley Authority			
455-00-4110 Tennessee Valley Authority Fund			
Nondefense Mandatory Administrative expenses in otherwise exempt resources	455	5.1	23
United States Court of Appeals for Veterans Claims			
345-00-0300 Salaries and Expenses			
Nondefense Discretionary Appropriation	31	5.0	2
United States Holocaust Memorial Museum			
456-00-3300 Holocaust Memorial Museum			
Nondefense Discretionary Appropriation	51	5.0	3
United States Institute of Peace			
458-00-1300 Operating Expenses			
Nondefense Discretionary Appropriation	39	5.0	2
United States Interagency Council on Homelessness			
376-00-1300 United States Interagency Council on the Homelessness			
Nondefense Discretionary Appropriation	3	5.0	*
Vietnam Education Foundation			

* denotes $500,000 or less.

Sequestrable Budgetary Resources and Reductions in Sequestrable Resources by OMB Account -- FY 2013

(Amounts in millions)

Agency / Bureau / Account / Function / BEA Category / Budgetary Resource	Sequestrable BA Amount	Sequester Percentage	Sequester Amount
519-00-5365 Vietnam Debt Repayment Fund			
Nondefense Mandatory Appropriation	5	5.1	*

Sequestrable Budgetary Resources and Reductions in Sequestrable Resources by OMB Account -- FY 2013
(Amounts in millions)

Agency / Bureau / Account / Function / BEA Category / Budgetary Resource	Sequestrable BA Amount	Sequester Percentage	Sequester Amount

Amounts may not sum to total due to rounding.

Mandatory Federal administrative expenses of otherwise exempt accounts are sequestrable pursuant to section 251A(8) and section 256(h) of BBEDCA.

Pursuant to section 255(f) of BBEDCA, the President notified the Congress of his decision to exempt all military personnel accounts from sequester for FY 2013. See the July 31, 2012 letter to the Congress, available at http://www.whitehouse.gov/sites/default/files/omb/legislative/letters/military-personnel-letter-biden.pdf.

Unobligated balances of budget authority carried over from prior fiscal years in defense function 050 accounts are sequestrable.

For intragovernmental payments, sequestration is applied to the paying account. The funds are generally exempt in the receiving account in accordance with section 255(g)(1)(A) of BBEDCA so that the same dollars are not sequestered twice.